200
FOUR-INGREDIENT
RECIPES

200
FOUR-INGREDIENT
RECIPES

fabulous, fast recipes with
only four ingredients

JOANNA FARROW

HERMES
HOUSE

This edition is published by Hermes House, an imprint of Anness Publishing Ltd, Hermes House, 88–89 Blackfriars Road, London SE1 8HA; tel. 020 7401 2077; fax 020 7633 9499

www.hermeshouse.com; www.annesspublishing.com

If you like the images in this book and would like to investigate using them for publishing, promotions or advertising, please visit our website www.practicalpictures.com for more information.

A CIP catalogue record for this book is available from the British Library.

Publisher: Joanna Lorenz
Managing Editor: Linda Fraser
Senior Editor: Susannah Blake
Copy Editor: Bridget Jones
Editorial Reader: Richard McGinlay
Production Controller: Steve Lang
Photography: Tim Auty, Martin Brigdale, Nicky Dowey, Gus Filgate, Michelle Garrett, Amanda Heywood, William Lingwood, Craig Robertson, Simon Smith
Recipes: Alex Barker, Jacqueline Clark, Joanna Farrow, Brian Glover, Jane Milton, Jennie Shapter, Marlena Spieler, Kate Whiteman

ETHICAL TRADING POLICY
At Anness Publishing we believe that business should be conducted in an ethical and ecologically sustainable way, with respect for the environment and a proper regard to the replacement of the natural resources we employ.
As a publisher, we use a lot of wood pulp to make high-quality paper for printing, and that wood commonly comes from spruce trees. We are therefore currently growing more than 750,000 trees in three Scottish forest plantations: Berrymoss (130 hectares/320 acres), West Touxhill (125 hectares/305 acres) and Deveron Forest (75 hectares/185 acres). The forests we manage contain more than 3.5 times the number of trees employed each year in making paper for the books we manufacture.
Because of this ongoing ecological investment programme, you, as our customer, can have the pleasure and reassurance of knowing that a tree is being cultivated on your behalf to naturally replace the materials used to make the book you are holding.
Our forestry programme is run in accordance with the UK Woodland Assurance Scheme (UKWAS) and will be certified by the internationally recognized Forest Stewardship Council (FSC). The FSC is a non-government organization dedicated to promoting responsible management of the world's forests. Certification ensures forests are managed in an environmentally sustainable and socially responsible way. For further information about this scheme, go to www.annesspublishing.com/trees

NOTES

Bracketed terms are intended for American readers.

For all recipes, quantities are given in both metric and imperial measures and, where appropriate, measures are also given in standard cups and spoons. Follow one set, but not a mixture, because they are not interchangeable.

Standard spoon and cup measures are level.

1 tsp = 5ml, 1 tbsp = 15ml, 1 cup = 250ml/8fl oz

Australian standard tablespoons are 20ml. Australian readers should use 3 tsp in place of 1 tbsp for measuring small quantities of gelatine, flour, salt, etc.

Medium (US large) eggs are used unless otherwise stated.

The very young, elderly and those in ill-health or with a compromised immune system are advised against consuming raw eggs or dishes containing raw eggs.

Contents

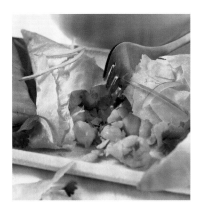

The Minimalist Approach

In recent years, cooking and eating trends have changed considerably, with more emphasis on dishes that are quick and easy to prepare, yet that are still exciting, sophisticated and delicious. This book teaches you how to really make the most of food – with simple, fabulous recipes that use only four ingredients, or less. Using a limited number of top-quality ingredients allows you to really savour the aroma, taste and texture of a dish and saves time on writing lists and shopping for ingredients. It also allows for fuss-free preparation, giving you more time to sit back, relax and enjoy.

When you're cooking with four ingredients, each one has to be a star player. It is important to buy the best-quality ingredients you can find so be selective when buying, as the better the raw materials, the more flavour the finished dish will have. Top-quality produce will also need fewer additional seasonings or flavourings to make them taste fabulous. Buying the best does not necessarily mean paying more. For example meat from a good, traditional-style butcher is often cheaper than the better-quality types in the supermarket and it will probably have a fuller flavour. Good fish can be slightly harder to find. Be particularly choosy when buying from supermarket fish counters: avoid tired-looking specimens and remember that it is better to go for good-quality frozen fish and shellfish rather than poor-quality fresh. Farmers' market stores can be great sources of good-quality fruit and vegetables, often at a good price, even for the more exotic produce.

Ready-made stocks and sauces are infinitely useful for creating quick and easy meals and are a great way to cut down on preparation and cooking time. A basic tomato sauce can lay the foundations for hundreds of different dishes such as stews, casseroles and pasta dishes. Simply

add poultry, meat, fish, vegetables or pulses and flavour with fresh herbs and spices. Sauces such as pesto are great for adding flavour, while a really great ready-made custard can be the perfect base for an ice cream. Good-quality bought sauces are readily available fresh or in jars – check out the list of ingredients on the pack for some indication of the quality. A good bought liquid concentrate or fresh stock is worth keeping in the refrigerator or freezer. Remember that many bought chilled fresh products are suitable for home freezing, which is a good way of extending their shelf life. Alternatively, you can make your own supply of basic stocks and sauces and freeze them in practical, ready-to-use batches.

Choosing really fresh, good-quality ingredients will help you to create delicious, flavoursome dishes.

Fresh herbs go perfectly with other simple flavours and play an essential role in minimalist cooking.

Adding a splash of robust wine or herb-infused vinegar to a sauce or stew can help to give extra body and flavour.

Storecupboard essentials

Try to avoid overstocking the storecupboard (pantry). Choose good-quality extra-virgin olive oil and balsamic vinegar for dressings and a lighter oil such as sunflower oil for cooking. A nut oil such as walnut or hazelnut is an interesting alternative to olive oil in salad dressings. One or two flavoured oils are great for adding extra taste.

Preserved or dried vegetables such as sun-dried tomatoes, bottled roasted (bell) peppers and capers have a powerful taste and can be useful for boosting flavour in many Mediterranean-style dishes. Dried mushrooms bring a full flavour to mushroom dishes and can be good for perking up simple soups, stews, casseroles and risottos.

Keep herb and spice supplies to a minimum as both lose their flavour comparatively quickly, particularly if exposed to light and warmth. If possible, it is better to grow or buy fresh herbs and freeze any leftovers for future use rather than stocking a cupboard full of dried spices that have an inferior flavour. If possible, stock whole spices such as cumin and coriander and grind them using a mortar and pestle or in a spice grinder as required as ground spices tend to lose their flavour quickly. Freshly grated whole nutmeg is better than ready ground and it adds interest to potato dishes and white sauces.

Other essential storecupboard (pantry) ingredients include salt and ground black pepper, sugar, plain (all-purpose) flour and cornflour (cornstarch), plus basic staples such as pasta and rice. It is also handy to have a small selection of condiments or sauces such as soy sauce or pesto that can help to perk up or enhance the flavour of simple dishes.

Rich-tasting anchovies are a perfect ingredient to keep in the storecupboard.

Using the recipes

Each recipe uses no more than four ingredients, excluding salt, pepper and water. Some recipes use ready-made stock or sauce – but you can always use a homemade one if you prefer. Serving suggestions and ideas for garnishes or decorations are included where appropriate, but these are not essential for the success of the dish. There are also suggestions for variations that offer alternative or additional flavourings and handy cook's tips that will help you achieve successful results every time.

Equipment

Having the right equipment makes cooking both easier and more enjoyable; chopping ingredients with a blunt knife simply becomes laborious. There are only a few items of really vital equipment. Knives, pans, mixing bowls, wooden spoons, roasting and baking tins (pans), measuring jugs (pitchers), whisks and sieves are all essential and the following are some items to which it is worth paying special attention. Many so-called labour-saving gadgets are, more often than not, used once or twice and then put away, cluttering up storage space.

Knives

Always buy good-quality knives. Although they are quite expensive, they will last for years, so buy them as you can afford them to build up a small set. Store knives in a knife rack or wallet for safety and to protect the blades. Blades should be sharpened frequently for good performance.

A good-quality knife is essential for preparing ingredients.

Chopping board

When chopping meat or fish, always use a plastic board and scrub well after use. However, a large, heavy sturdy wooden board is a good choice for preparing vegetables and fruit as it will not slip while in use. Avoid glass boards as they blunt knives very quickly.

Pans

Three or four different-sized pans are ample for most households. Choose heavy pans as they do not burn easily when making sauces and long-simmered dishes.

Frying pans

One large, heavy stainless steel frying pan, preferably with a lid, is sufficient in most kitchens. However, a non-stick pan is essential for dry-frying foods or for cooking in a very small amount of oil.

Wok

Even if you do not do much stir-frying or Asian-style cooking, a wok is useful for a variety of other cooking methods such as cooking and tossing pasta dishes, vegetables, tomato sauces and any other ingredients that might normally spill out of a traditional frying pan.

Weighing scales

These are useful if you make breads, cakes or any dishes requiring accurate quantities for success. There are a wide variety of different scales available from spring and balance scales to digital scales, which can be extremely accurate.

Measuring spoons

A set of metal measuring spoons is essential as table cutlery can vary widely in volume, making spoons intended for eating or serving food unsuitable for measuring quanitities.

A set of measuring spoons is a small, worthwhile investment.

Measuring jugs and cups

Heatproof jugs (pitchers) marked with metric and imperial measurements are useful for measuring liquids. Cups, which vary in size from $1/4$–1 cup, are used in several countries to measure wet and dry ingredients.

Electrical equipment

Food processors are the most useful of all the electrical appliances, as they take the effort out of chopping, blending,

A goblet blender is perfect for making drinks and soups.

grating and making pastes and purées. Some large food processors have smaller containers that fit inside the large bowl for processing smaller quantities. A blender wand or hand-held blender that processes ingredients in a pan is especially useful and, like a goblet blender, it reduces soups to a finer texture than a food processor. An electric whisk is practical for whipping cream, whisking egg whites and creaming cakes.

Cooking techniques

Allowing onions to brown caramelizes their surface and adds flavour to the final dish.

When using a limited number of ingredients, straightforward, flavour-enhancing cooking methods are the best choice. Frying, grilling (broiling) and roasting can help to enrich the ingredients, causing caramelization and browning on the surface. The cooked food will be well flavoured, needing little more than lemon wedges or a simple condiment to complete the dish. Steaming is quite different – highlighting the natural flavour of ingredients. Minimum seasonings are necessary but subtle sauces can enhance the plain cooked foods. Concentrating on simple cooking methods helps to keep the core recipe quick and easy.

Frying

This is good for enriching the natural flavour of ingredients. There are several methods: deep-frying, pan-frying or shallow-frying, stir-frying and dry-frying. Each one uses different quantities of fat and produces different results.

The initial frying of ingredients can help to determine the final character of a dish. Heat the oil before adding the ingredients and do not add too much to the pan at once. Overfilling the pan will steam or braise, rather than fry, the food, which will affect the final flavour. If necessary, fry ingredients in batches.

Stir-frying uses less oil than traditional frying methods and combines all the ingredients in one pan, bringing together a few complementary flavours. The juices yielded in stir-frying are usually sufficient to form a sauce. Dry-frying in a non-stick pan requires no fat so is ideal when trying to reduce the number of cooking ingredients.

Deep-frying can bring out rich flavours in simple ingredients.

Grilling

Cooking under a grill (broiler) or on a griddle can really bring out the flavour of good quality ingredients, imparting a rich, smoky flavour. Meat, poultry, fish, shellfish and vegetables need little more than light seasoning and brushing with oil. Time permitting, the food can be marinated in advance in a bought marinade or simple mixture of lemon juice or wine,

Cooking on a griddle is quick and easy and produces delicious, attractive results.

garlic and herbs. Preheat the grill before cooking the food and baste non-fatty foods with oil, marinade or a basting mixture during grilling to prevent them from drying out.

Roasting

Traditionally a method used for cooking meat and poultry, roasting is also excellent for large pieces of fish and vegetables. The ingredients are cooked uncovered to encourage browning and the formation of a crisp and golden surface. When temperature and timing are correct the foods stay moist and succulent inside. Basting with butter or olive oil, or

Chicken is delicious roasted with simple aromatic flavours such as garlic and herbs.

juices that seep out during cooking, helps to flavour and crisp the skin as well as keep the food moist.

Steaming

This simple cooking method focuses on the natural, raw, taste of the food. Cooking in steam does not impart flavour in the way that frying, grilling (broiling) and roasting can so it is best used for cooking ingredients that have an excellent natural flavour, which can be savoured plain or served with an interesting sauce or accompaniment. Steaming is a gentle method that produces wonderfully moist results and is perfectly suited to vegetables and fish. Check food frequently during steaming as some foods cook surprisingly quickly.

Making Basic Stocks

A well-flavoured stock is particularly good in dishes that rely on minimal ingredients. Good-quality ready-made stocks – either cube, powders or liquid concentrate – are readily available but stocks are easy and cheap to make. Always ask for the meat bones when buying from a butcher and trimmings if you have fish prepared by the fishmonger as these are perfect for making good stock. A chicken carcass from a roast makes excellent stock, particularly if you've packed it with herbs, onions, garlic or other aromatics before roasting. A good vegetable stock can be made from trimmings when preparing vegetables and small quantities of leftover produce. Leave the onion skins on if you want a rich, dark-coloured stock.

Beef Stock   MAKES ABOUT 1 LITRE/1¾ PINTS/4 CUPS

900g/2lb beef bones

2 unpeeled onions, quartered

1 bouquet garni

2 large carrots, roughly chopped

1 Preheat the oven to 220°C/425°F/Gas 7. Put the beef bones in a roasting pan and roast for about 45 minutes, or until well browned.

2 Transfer the roasted bones to a large, heavy pan. Add the onion quarters, leaving the skins on, the bouquet garni and chopped carrots. Add 5ml/1 tsp salt and 5ml/1 tsp black peppercorns. Pour over about 1.7 litres/3 pints/7½ cups cold water and bring just to the boil.

3 Using a slotted spoon, skim off any scum on the surface of the stock. Reduce the heat and partially cover the pan. Simmer the stock on the lowest heat for about 3 hours, then set aside to cool slightly.

4 Strain the stock into a large bowl and leave to cool completely, then remove any fat from the surface. Store the stock in the refrigerator for up to 3 days or freeze for up to 6 months.

Chicken Stock   MAKES ABOUT 1 LITRE/1¾ PINTS/4 CUPS

1 large roast chicken carcass

2 unpeeled onions, quartered

3 bay leaves

2 large carrots, roughly chopped

1 Put the chicken carcass and any loose bones and roasting juices into a heavy pan in which they fit snugly. Add the onion quarters, bay leaves and chopped carrots.

2 Add 2.5ml/½ tsp salt and 5ml/1 tsp black peppercorns to the pan, and pour over 1.7 litres/3 pints/7½ cups cold water. Bring just to the boil.

3 Reduce the heat, partially cover the pan and cook on the lowest setting for about 1½ hours. Using a large spoon, carefully turn the chicken in the stock and crush the carcass occasionally.

4 Leave the stock to cool slightly, then strain into a large bowl and leave to cool completely. When cool, remove any fat from the surface. Store the stock in the refrigerator for up to 2 days or freeze for up to 6 months.

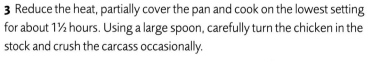

Fish Stock MAKES ABOUT 600ML/1 PINT/2½ CUPS

500g/1¼lb fish bones and trimmings, without heads and gills

1 bouquet garni

1 onion or 3–4 shallots, peeled and quartered

2 celery sticks, roughly chopped

1 Pack the fish bones and trimmings into a heavy pan and add the bouquet garni, quartered onion or shallots and celery.

2 Add 2.5ml/½ tsp salt and 2.5ml/½ tsp peppercorns to the pan and pour over 1 litre/1¾ pints/4 cups water. Bring to the boil.

3 Reduce the heat, partially cover the pan and cook on the lowest setting for about 30 minutes, stirring occasionally. Leave to cool slightly, then strain into a bowl and cool completely. Store in the refrigerator for up to 24 hours or freeze for up to 3 months.

Vegetable Stock MAKES ABOUT 1 LITRE/1¾ PINTS/4 CUPS

3 unpeeled onions, quartered

200g/7oz large open mushrooms

300–400g/11–14oz mixed vegetables, such as broccoli, carrots, celery, tomatoes and/or spring onions (scallions), roughly chopped

45ml/3 tbsp green or brown lentils

1 Place the onions in a heavy pan with the mushrooms, mixed vegetables and green or brown lentils.

2 Add 2.5ml/½ tsp salt, 10ml/2 tsp peppercorns and 1.7 litres/3 pints/7½ cups water to the pan. Bring to the boil, then reduce the heat and simmer, partially covered, for 50–60 minutes.

3 Leave the stock to cool slightly, then strain into a bowl and leave to cool. Store in the refrigerator for up to 24 hours or freeze for up to 6 months.

Bouquet Garni

This little bundle of herbs is perfect for adding flavour to stocks, soups and stews. Tying the herbs in a bundle means that the bouquet garni is easy to remove after cooking. A traditional bouquet garni comprises sprigs of parsley, thyme and a bay leaf, but you can vary the herbs according to the dish and/or main ingredients. Rosemary and oregano are good with lamb, while mint, chervil, basil, chives and tarragon go well with fish.

1 Using a short length of string, tie together a bay leaf and sprigs of thyme and parsley.

2 Alternatively, place the herbs in the centre of a square of muslin (cheesecloth) and tie into a neat bundle using a short length of string.

3 Use the bouquet garni immediately or freeze, ready for cooking. (Herbs tied in muslin are better suited to freezing than bundles simply tied with string.)

FREEZING STOCK

The main ingredients for stock can be frozen – meat bones, fish trimmings or a cooked chicken carcass – ready to make home-made stock at a later date.

More conveniently, stock itself freezes very well. Once the stock has been strained and the fat removed, reduce the volume by boiling the stock uncovered. This concentrates its flavour and takes up less freezer space. A highly reduced stock, boiled to a thick syrup, can be frozen in an ice cube tray. Make a note of the volume before boiling, then add this to the label when packing the stock for the freezer. This way you will know how much water to add when the concentrated stock is thawed.

Making Basic Savoury Sauces

A good sauce can provide the finishing touch for a dish. There are a large number of ready-made sauces available, but they are also very easy to make yourself. One of the most basic sauces is the classic savoury white sauce, which can be served as a simple topping for vegetables or flavoured with additional ingredients such as cheese, herbs, onions or mushrooms and served with pasta, fish or poultry. A basic fresh tomato sauce is widely used for pasta dishes, pizza toppings and vegetable dishes and it is worth making when ripe tomatoes are available. It can be stored in the refrigerator for several days or can be frozen for up to 6 months. Hollandaise sauce is another classic accompaniment for fish and vegetables. Unlike the other sauces it cannot be made ahead, but it it is available commercially.

White Sauce MAKES ABOUT 300ML/½ PINT/1¼ CUPS

300ml/½ pint/1¼ cups milk

15g/½oz/1 tbsp butter

15g/½oz plain (all-purpose) flour

freshly grated nutmeg

1 Warm the milk in a small pan. In a separate pan, melt the butter over a gently heat, then add the flour and cook, stirring, for 1 minute until the mixture forms a thick paste.

2 Remove the pan from the heat and gradually add the warmed milk, whisking continuously until smooth.

3 Return the pan to a gentle heat and cook, whisking, until the sauce boils, is smooth and thickened. Season with salt and freshly ground pepper and plenty of nutmeg.

Fresh Tomato Sauce MAKES ABOUT 1 LITRE/1¾ PINTS/4 CUPS

1.3kg/3lb ripe tomatoes

120ml/4fl oz/½ cup garlic-infused olive oil

1 large onion, finely chopped

small handful of basil leaves, torn, or 30ml/2 tbsp chopped fresh oregano

1 Put the tomatoes in a bowl, pour over boiling water to cover and leave to stand for about 1 minute until the skins split. Drain and peel, then roughly chop the flesh.

2 Heat half the oil in a large heavy pan. Add the chopped onion and cook gently for about 3 minutes, or until softened but not browned.

3 Add the tomatoes and the remaining oil to the pan and cook gently, stirring, for 5 minutes, or until the tomatoes are soft and juicy.

4 Add the herbs, cover and cook gently for 20–25 minutes, stirring frequently, until the sauce is thickened and pulpy. Season to taste.

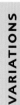

VARIATIONS

• *Try using different herbs such as flat leaf parsley, marjoram, thyme, rosemary or coriander (cilantro) in place of the basil or oregano.*

• *To make a warm, mildly peppery sauce add a little paprika or, to make a spicy sauce, add a little chilli powder (or a finely chopped fresh chilli).*

• *To make a much more garlicky sauce, add 2–3 crushed garlic cloves to the pan just before adding the chopped tomatoes.*

Hollandaise Sauce MAKES ABOUT 120ML/4FL OZ/½ CUP

45ml/3 tbsp white wine or herb-infused vinegar

1 bay leaf

2 egg yolks

115g/4oz/½ cup butter, chilled

COOK'S TIP *The sauce can be kept warm in a covered bowl set over the pan of hot water for up to 20 minutes. If the sauce is very thick, whisk in a few drops of hot water. If the sauce starts to separate, whisk in an ice cube.*

1 Put the vinegar in a small pan with the bay leaf and add 5ml/ 1 tsp black peppercorns. Boil rapidly until reduced to 15ml/ 1 tsp, then strain into a heatproof bowl.

2 Put the vinegar in a clean pan, add the egg yolks and a little salt and whisk lightly until thoroughly combined. Cut the chilled butter into small pieces.

3 Add the butter to the pan and set the pan over a very low heat. Whisk continuously so that as the butter melts it is blended into the egg yolks. When all the butter has melted, continue whisking until the sauce is thick and smooth.

4 Season the sauce with salt and ground black pepper to taste, adding a few extra drops of vinegar, if you like, to give a slightly tangy flavour. Serve warm.

Mayonnaise MAKES 150ML/¼ PINT/⅔ CUP

1 egg yolk, at room temperature

15ml/1 tbsp lemon juice or white wine vinegar

5ml/1 tsp Dijon mustard

150ml/¼ pint/⅔ cup olive oil

1 Put the egg yolk in a bowl with the lemon juice or vinegar, mustard and a little salt. Whisk together until combined.

2 Gradually add the oil in a thin trickle, whisking continuously until the sauce is thickened and smooth. This will take several minutes.

3 Check the seasoning, adding a few drops of lemon juice or vinegar if the mayonnaise is too bland. If the sauce is too thick, stir in a few drops of warm water. Cover with clear film (plastic wrap) and store in the refrigerator for up to 2 days.

Flavoured Oils

There are plenty of flavoured oils available in delicatessens and supermarkets, infused (steeped) with aromatics such as lemon, garlic, herbs and chillies, which are delicious served as a simple dressing for freshly cooked pasta or a salad. Home-made versions are less expensive and you can be more selective with the flavours you choose. Once made, the oil should be left in a cool place for up to a week to allow the flavours to infuse. Then the oil should be strained before storing. The aromatic ingredients should not be stored long term in the oil, because of the risk of harmful moulds developing.

Basil Oil Blend a large handful of basil leaves with 200ml/7fl oz/scant 1 cup olive oil in a food processor. Leave overnight, then strain through a muslin- (cheesecloth-) lined sieve into a clean bowl. Store in the refrigerator, then bring to room temperature before using.

Garlic and Rosemary Oil Put a handful of rosemary sprigs in a pan with 3 sliced garlic cloves and 120ml/4fl oz/½ cup olive oil. Heat gently until bubbling, then pour into a heatproof bowl, cover and leave in a cool place overnight. Strain the garlic and rosemary oil into a clean 300–400ml/10–14fl oz/1¼–1⅔ cup bottle and top up with more oil.

Making Basic Sweet Sauces

From creamy, comforting custard to an elegant fruit coulis, sweet sauces can be used to uplift the simplest puddings and desserts to create a truly spectacular dish. They can be served as an accompaniment or make up an intrinsic part of a dish. Simple vanilla ice cream is taken to new levels when served with hot chocolate sauce or a fresh raspberry coulis, while a classic vanilla custard can be used as the base of a sweet soufflé. These sweet sauces rely on just a few basic ingredients and minimal effort, producing irresistible results. The dessert sauce can be made in advance, before serving the meal, ready for reheating or serving cold. Even custard can be re-heated, just take care to use very gentle heat to prevent it from curdling.

Real Custard MAKES 300ML/½ PINT/1¼ CUPS

300ml/½ pint/1¼ cups full-cream (whole) milk or half milk and half double (heavy) cream

3 egg yolks

5ml/1 tsp cornflour (cornstarch)

45ml/3 tbsp caster (superfine) sugar or vanilla sugar

1 Pour the milk or milk and cream mixture into a double boiler or heavy pan and bring slowly to the boil over a very gentle heat.

2 Meanwhile, whisk the egg yolks with the cornflour and sugar until thoroughly mixed. Pour the boiled milk into the yolk mixture, whisking continuously until combined.

3 Pour the mixture back into the cleaned pan and cook over the lowest heat, stirring continuously with a wooden spoon, for 8–10 minutes, or until the mixture coats the back of the spoon.

4 Immediately pour the custard through a sieve into a bowl or jug (pitcher) to prevent it from overcooking. Serve warm.

> **COOK'S TIP** *Always cook custard over the lowest heat possible to reduce the risk of curdling. Adding a little cornflour to the sauce helps to prevent it from curdling without affecting the consistency or flavour.*

Summer Fruit Coulis MAKES ABOUT 250ML/8FL OZ/1 CUP

130g/4½oz raspberries

130g/4½oz strawberries

10–15ml/2–3 tsp icing (confectioners') sugar

15ml/1 tbsp orange liqueur or Kirsch (optional)

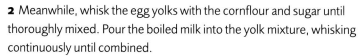
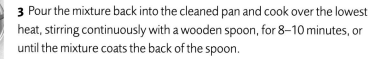

1 Place the raspberries and strawberries in a food processor and process until smooth. Press the mixture through a fine strainer set over a bowl to remove the tiny seeds.

2 Return the strained fruit purée to the food processor or blender and add 10ml/2 tsp of the icing sugar with the orange liqueur or kirsch, if using, and process briefly until well combined.

3 Check the sweetness of the coulis, then add a little more icing sugar if necessary and process again to mix.

Rich Chocolate Sauce MAKES ABOUT 250ML/8FL OZ/1 CUP

130g/4½oz caster (superfine) sugar

175g/6oz plain (semisweet) chocolate, broken into pieces

25g/1oz/2 tbsp unsalted (sweet) butter

30ml/2 tbsp brandy or coffee liqueur (optional)

1 Put the sugar in a small heavy pan with 120ml/4fl oz/½ cup water and heat gently until the sugar dissolves. Bring to the boil and boil for 1 minute.

2 Remove from the heat and stir in the chocolate and butter, stirring until the chocolate has melted and the sauce is smooth.

3 Stir in the brandy or coffee liqueur, if using, and serve warm.

Rosemary and Almond Cream MAKES ABOUT 600ML/1 PINT/2½ CUPS

This deliciously fragrant cream is more of an accompaniment than a sauce and is an excellent alternative to plain whipped cream served with fruit compotes, pies and tarts or a bowl of fresh fruits. Rosemary works really well (particularly if you then decorate the dish with flowering sprigs) but bay leaves or thyme sprigs also provide a lovely flavour.

300ml/½ pint/1¼ cups double (heavy) cream

2 rosemary sprigs

25g/1oz/½ cup finely ground amaretti or macaroon biscuits

15ml/1 tbsp almond liqueur such as amaretto (optional)

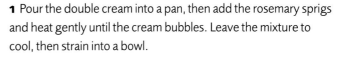

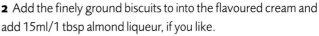

1 Pour the double cream into a pan, then add the rosemary sprigs and heat gently until the cream bubbles. Leave the mixture to cool, then strain into a bowl.

2 Add the finely ground biscuits to into the flavoured cream and add 15ml/1 tbsp almond liqueur, if you like.

3 Whisk the cream and crushed biscuits together until the mixture is just holding its shape, then transfer to a serving dish and chill until ready to serve.

Flavoured Sugar

A store of herb-and spice-infused (-steeped) sugars provides plenty of flavouring options for sauces, desserts and cakes without the need for additional ingredients. Vanilla sugar is the best known and can be bought easily, but there are many other equally useful flavours. Use in any recipe instead of ordinary sugar or use half flavoured and half ordinary sugar.

Vanilla Sugar Half fill a small jar with white or golden caster (superfine) sugar and add 1 vanilla pod (bean). Top up with sugar, seal and store in a cool place for a week before using.

Spice Sugar Half fill a small jar with caster (superfine) sugar and add either 2 broken cinnamon sticks, 15ml/1 tbsp lightly bruised cardamom pods, or 4 star anise and top up with more sugar. Seal and store in a cool dark place for about a week before using.

Flower or Herb Sugar Half fill a small jar with caster (superfine) sugar and add either a handful of fresh, dry rose petals; several sprigs of lavender, rosemary or thyme; or several bay leaves. Shake gently to distribute the flowers or herbs and top up with more sugar, seal and store in a cool dark place for about a week before using.

Juices and Drinks

FRESHLY MADE FRUIT AND VEGETABLE JUICES CAN ACT AS
A REFRESHING, REVITALIZING TONIC, WHILE FROTHY HOT
CHOCOLATE OR VANILLA CAFFÈ LATTE CAN BE A RELAXING,
INDULGENT TREAT. THIS CHAPTER IS PACKED WITH EASY-
TO-MAKE DRINKS THAT CAN BE SIPPED AT LEISURE OR
ENJOYED AS A PICK-ME-UP WHEN SPIRITS ARE FLAGGING.

Leafy Apple Lift-off

This delicious blend of fruit and fresh green leaves is refreshing and healthy. The leaves are robustly flavoured and have a peppery, pungent taste. To prepare the leaves, discard any damaged and discoloured ones and rinse thoroughly in cold water to remove any grit. To prevent the juice from being watery, dry the leaves in a salad spinner or on kitchen paper before juicing.

SERVES ONE

1 Quarter the apple. Using a juice extractor, juice the fruit and watercress, rocket or spinach.

2 Add the lime juice to the apple, grape and leaf mixture and stir thoroughly to blend all the ingredients together. Pour the juice into a tall glass and serve immediately.

1 eating apple

150g/5oz white grapes

25g/1oz watercress, rocket (arugula) or spinach

15ml/1 tbsp lime juice

Fennel Fusion

The hearty combination of raw vegetables and apples makes a surprisingly delicious juice that is packed with natural goodness and is a truly wonderful pick-me-up. Use the remaining cabbage and fennel to make a really crunchy salad – slice and dress with French dressing or simply with olive oil, herb vinegar and plenty of freshly ground black pepper and sea salt to taste.

SERVES ONE

1 Coarsely slice the red cabbage and the fennel bulb and quarter the eating apples. Using a juice extractor, juice the vegetables and fruit.

2 Add the lemon juice to the red cabbage, fennel and apple mixture and stir thoroughly to blend all the ingredients together. Pour into a glass and serve immediately.

½ small red cabbage

½ fennel bulb

2 eating apples

15ml/1 tbsp lemon juice

Tropical Calm

This deliciously scented juice is packed with goodness to cleanse and calm the system. Orange fruits such as cantaloupe melons and papayas are rich in the phytochemical betacarotene, which is a valuable antioxidant and is thought to have many health-promoting properties.

SERVES ONE

1 papaya

½ cantaloupe melon

90g/3½oz seedless white grapes

1 Halve the papaya, remove the seeds and skin, then cut the flesh into coarse slices. Halve the melon, remove the seeds, cut into quarters, slice the flesh away from the skin and cut into chunks.

2 Using a juicer, juice the prepared fruit. Alternatively, blend the fruit in a food processor or blender for a thicker juice. Serve immediately.

Strawberry Soother

Relax with this comforting blend of just two fruits – it is rich in vitamin C and fabulous flavour. It's a perfect drink for summer when sweet strawberries, peaches and necatarines are in season.

SERVES ONE

225g/8oz/2 cups strawberries

1 peach or nectarine

1 Hull the strawberries. Using a sharp knife, quarter the peach or nectarine and pull out the stone (pit). Cut the flesh into coarse slices or chunks.

2 Using a juice extractor, juice the fruit. Alternatively, place the fruit in a food processor or blender and process until smooth. Serve immediately.

Carrot Revitalizer

This vibrant combination of vegetables and fruit makes a lively, health-giving drink. Carrots yield generous quantities of sweet juice, which goes perfectly with the sharp flavour of pear and the zesty taste of orange. This powerful drink will nourish and stimulate the system.

SERVES ONE

1 Scrub and trim the carrots and quarter the apples. Peel the orange and cut into rough segments.

2 Using a juice extractor, juice the carrots and fruit, pour into a glass and serve immediately.

3 carrots

2 apples

1 orange

Purple Pep

Jewel-coloured beetroot juice is well known for its detoxifying properties so this juice makes the perfect choice when you've been over-doing it. It offers an excellent supply of valuable nutrients that are essential for good health.

SERVES ONE

3 carrots

115g/4oz beetroot (beet)

25g/1oz baby spinach, washed and dried

2 celery sticks

1 Scrub and trim the carrots and beetroot. Using a sharp knife, cut the beetroot into large chunks.

2 Using a juice extractor, juice the carrots, beetroot, spinach and celery, then pour into a glass and serve immediately.

Melon Pick-me-up

Spicy fresh root ginger is delicious with melon and pear in this reviving and invigorating concoction. Charentais or Galia melon can be used instead of the cantaloupe melon in this recipe. To enjoy fresh root ginger at its best, buy it in small quantities and keep in a cool, dry place for up to a week. As it ages, the root will dry out and become hard.

SERVES ONE

1 Quarter the cantaloupe melon, remove the seeds using a teaspoon or a sharp knife, and carefully slice the flesh away from the skin, reserving any juice. Quarter the pears and reserve any juice.

2 Using a juice extractor, juice the melon flesh and juice, quartered pears and juice and the fresh root ginger. Pour the juice into a tall glass and serve immediately.

½ **cantaloupe melon**

2 pears

2.5cm/1in piece of fresh root ginger

Apple Shiner

This refreshing fusion of sweet apple, honeydew melon, red grapes and lemon provides a reviving burst of energy and a feel-good sensation. Serve as a drink or use to pour over muesli (granola) for a quick and healthy breakfast.

SERVES ONE

1 eating apple

½ **honeydew melon**

90g/3½oz red grapes

15ml/1 tbsp lemon juice

1 Quarter the apple and remove the core. Cut the melon into quarters, remove the seeds and slice the flesh away from the skin.

2 Using a juice extractor, juice the apple, melon and grapes. Alternatively, process the fruit in a food processor or blender for 2–3 minutes, until smooth. Pour the juice into a long, tall glass, stir in the lemon juice and serve immediately.

Citrus Sparkle

Zesty citrus fruits are packed with vitamin C, which is necessary for a healthy immune system. Pink grapefruit have a sweeter flavour than the yellow varieties – in fact, the pinker they are, the sweeter they are likely to be. For a lighter drink to serve two, divide the juice between two glasses and top up with sparkling mineral water or soda water (club soda) and ice cubes.

SERVES ONE

1 Cut the pink grapefruit and orange in half and squeeze out the juice using a citrus fruit squeezer.

2 Pour the juice into a glass, stir in 15ml/1 tbsp lemon juice, add the remaining lemon juice if required and serve immediately.

1 pink grapefruit

1 orange

30ml/2 tbsp freshly squeezed lemon juice

Hum-zinger

Aromatic tropical fruits make a drink that is bursting with flavour and energy. Enjoy a glass first thing in the morning to kick-start your day.

SERVES ONE

½ pineapple, peeled

1 small mango, peeled and stoned (pitted)

½ small papaya, seeded and peeled

1 Remove any "eyes" left in the pineapple, then cut all the fruit into fairly coarse chunks.

2 Using a juice extractor, juice the fruit. Alternatively, use a food processor or blender and process for about 2–3 minutes until smooth. Pour into a glass and serve immediately.

Honey and Watermelon Tonic

This refreshing juice will help to cool the body, calm the digestion and cleanse the system, and may even have aphrodisiac qualities. On hot days add ice cubes to keep the juice cool. The distinctive pinkish-red flesh of the watermelon gives this tonic a beautiful hue – decorate with a few fresh mint leaves to provide a stunning colour contrast.

SERVES FOUR

1 Cut the watermelon flesh into chunks, cutting away the skin and discarding the black seeds. Place in a large bowl, pour the chilled water over and leave to stand for 10 minutes.

2 Tip the mixture into a large sieve set over a bowl. Using a wooden spoon, press gently on the fruit to extract all the liquid.

3 Stir in the lime juice and sweeten to taste with honey. Pour into a jug (pitcher) or glasses and serve.

1 watermelon

1 litre/1¾ pints/ 4 cups chilled still mineral water

juice of 2 limes

clear honey, to taste

Cranberry, Ginger and Cinnamon Spritzer

Partially freezing fruit juice gives it a refreshingly slushy texture. The combination of cranberry and apple juice is tart and clean. Add a few fresh or frozen cranberries to decorate each glass, if you like.

SERVES FOUR

600ml/1 pint/2½ cups chilled cranberry juice

150ml/¼ pint/⅔ cup clear apple juice

4 cinnamon sticks

about 400ml/14fl oz/ 1⅔ cups chilled ginger ale

1 Pour the cranberry juice into a shallow freezerproof container and freeze for about 2 hours, or until a thick layer of ice crystals has formed around the edges.

2 Mash the semi-frozen juice with a fork to break up the ice, then return the mixture to the freezer for a further 2–3 hours or until it is almost solid.

3 Pour the apple juice into a small pan, add two cinnamon sticks and bring to just below boiling point. Pour into a jug (pitcher) and leave to cool, then remove the cinnamon sticks and set them aside. Cool, then chill the juice.

4 Spoon the cranberry ice into a food processor or blender. Add the cinnamon-flavoured apple juice and process briefly until slushy. Pile the mixture into cocktail glasses, top up with chilled ginger ale, decorate with cinnamon sticks and serve immediately.

Strawberry and Banana Smoothie

The blend of perfectly ripe bananas and strawberries creates a drink that is both fruity and creamy, with a luscious texture. Papaya, mango or pineapple can be used instead of strawberries for a tropical drink. Popular with adults and children alike, this is a great way to get children to enjoy fruit – much healthier than commercial milkshakes, too.

SERVES FOUR

200g/7oz/1¾ cups strawberries, plus extra, sliced, to decorate

2 ripe bananas

300ml/½ pint/1¼ cups skimmed milk

10 ice cubes

1 Hull the strawberries. Peel the bananas and chop them into fairly large chunks.

2 Put the fruit in a food processor or blender. Process to a thick, coarse purée, scraping down the sides of the goblet as necessary.

3 Add the skimmed milk and ice cubes, crushing the ice first unless you have a heavy-duty processor. Process until smooth and thick. Pour into tall glasses and top each with strawberry slices to decorate. Serve immediately.

EXTRAS *For a rich and velvety drink, add 120ml/ 4fl oz/½ cup coconut milk and process as above. Reduce the volume of milk to 175ml/6fl oz/¾ cup.*

Raspberry and Orange Smoothie

Sharp-sweet raspberries and zesty oranges taste fabulous combined with the light creaminess of yogurt. This smoothie takes just minutes to prepare, making it perfect for breakfast – or any other time of the day. If you like a really tangy drink add freshly squeezed lemon or lime juice to taste.

SERVES TWO TO THREE

1 Place the raspberries and yogurt in a food processor or blender and process for about 1 minute, until smooth and creamy.

2 Add the orange juice to the raspberry and yogurt mixture and process for about 30 seconds, or until thoroughly combined. Pour into tall glasses and serve immediately.

COOK'S TIP *For a super-chilled version, use frozen raspberries or a combination of frozen summer berries such as strawberries, redcurrants and blueberries instead of fresh. You may need to blend the raspberries and yogurt slightly longer for a really smooth result.*

250g/9oz/1½ cups fresh raspberries, chilled

200ml/7fl oz/scant 1 cup natural (plain) yogurt, chilled

300ml/½ pint/1¼ cups freshly squeezed orange juice, chilled

New York Egg Cream

No one knows precisely why this legendary drink is called egg cream, but some say it was a witty way of describing richness at a time when no one could afford to put both expensive eggs and cream together in a drink. Use full-fat (whole) milk for a really creamy taste. Dust a little cocoa powder over the top of the egg cream before serving, if you like.

SERVES ONE

45–60ml/3–4 tbsp good quality
chocolate syrup

120ml/4fl oz/½ cup chilled milk

175ml/6fl oz/¾ cup chilled
sparkling mineral water

1 Carefully pour the chocolate syrup into the bottom of a tall glass avoiding dripping any on the inside of the glass.

2 Pour the chilled milk into the glass on to the chocolate syrup.

3 Gradually pour the chilled sparkling mineral water into the glass, sip up any foam that rises to the top of the glass and carefully continue to add the remaining chilled sparkling mineral water. Stir well before drinking.

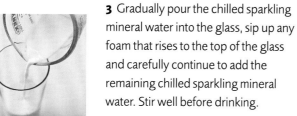

COOK'S TIP *An authentic egg cream is made with an old-fashioned seltzer dispenser that you press and spritz. In any case, you can use soda water (club soda) rather than mineral water, if you like.*

Banana and Maple Flip

This satisfying drink is packed with so much goodness that it makes a complete breakfast in a glass – great for when you're in a hurry. Be sure to use a really fresh free-range egg. The glass can be decorated with a slice of orange or lime to serve.

SERVES ONE

1 small banana, peeled and halved

50ml/2fl oz/¼ cup thick Greek (US strained plain) yogurt

1 egg

30ml/2 tbsp maple syrup

1 Put the peeled and halved banana, thick Greek yogurt, egg and maple syrup in a food processor or blender. Add 30ml/ 2 tbsp chilled water.

2 Process the ingredients constantly for about 2 minutes, or until the mixture turns a really pale, creamy colour and has a nice frothy texture.

3 Pour the banana and maple flip into a tall, chilled glass and serve immediately. Decorate the glasses with an orange or lime slice, if you like.

COOK'S TIPS

• *To chill the drinking glass quickly, place it in the freezer while you are preparing the drink.*

• *For a hint of sharpness, add 5ml/1 tsp lemon or lime juice or use a slightly tangy yogurt.*

Atole

This drink, rather like a thick milkshake in consistency, is made from Mexican cornflour (masa harina) and flavoured with piloncillo (Mexican unrefined brown sugar). Ground cinnamon and/or fresh fruit purées are often added before serving, and some recipes introduce ground almonds.

SERVES SIX

1 Combine the milk with 600ml/ 1 pint/2½ cups cold water. Put the masa harina in a heavy pan and gradually beat in the milk and water mixture to make a smooth paste.

2 Place the pan over a moderate heat, add the vanilla pod and bring the mixture to the boil, stirring constantly until it thickens. Beat in the sugar and stir until the sugar has dissolved. Remove from the heat, discard the vanilla and serve.

200g/7oz/1¾ cups white masa harina

600ml/1 pint/ 2½ cups milk

1 vanilla pod (bean)

50g/2oz/¼ cup piloncillo or soft dark brown sugar

EXTRAS

Process 115g/4oz/ 1 cup strawberries, chopped pineapple or orange segments in a food processor or blender until smooth, then press the purée through a sieve. Stir the purée into the corn mixture and return the pan to the heat until warmed through. Remove the vanilla pod and serve.

Café de Olla

This spiced black coffee is one of the most popular drinks in Mexico. The name means out of the pot, which refers to the heavy earthenware cooking pot, or *olla*, in which the coffee is made. Piloncillo is the local unrefined brown sugar, but any soft dark brown sugar can be used. French or Viennese roast coffees work particularly well in this hot drink.

SERVES FOUR

115g/4oz/½ cup piloncillo or soft dark brown sugar

4 cinnamon sticks, each about 15cm/ 6in long

50g/2oz/⅔ cup freshly ground coffee, from dark-roast coffee beans

1 Pour 1 litre/1¾ pints/4 cups water into a pan. Add the sugar and cinnamon sticks. Heat gently, stirring occasionally to make sure that the sugar dissolves, then bring to the boil. Boil rapidly for about 20 minutes, until the syrup has reduced by one-quarter.

2 Add the ground coffee to the syrup and stir well, then bring the liquid back to the boil. Remove from the heat, cover the pan and leave to stand for about 5 minutes.

3 Strain the coffee through a fine sieve. Pour into cups and serve.

Vanilla Caffè Latte

This luxurious vanilla and chocolate version of the classic coffee drink can be served at any time of the day topped with whipped cream, with cinnamon sticks to stir and flavour the drink. Caffè latte is a popular breakfast drink in Italy and France, and is now widely available elsewhere.

SERVES TWO

1 Pour the milk into a small pan and bring to the boil, then remove from the heat. Mix the espresso or very strong coffee with 500ml/16fl oz/ 2 cups of the boiled milk in a large heatproof jug (pitcher). Sweeten with vanilla sugar to taste.

2 Return the remaining boiled milk in the pan to the heat and add the 45ml/3 tbsp vanilla sugar. Stir constantly until dissolved. Bring to the boil, then reduce the heat. Add the dark chocolate and continue to heat, stirring constantly until all the chocolate has melted and the mixture is smooth and glossy.

3 Pour the chocolate milk into the jug of coffee and whisk thoroughly. Serve in tall mugs or glasses topped with whipped cream and with cinnamon sticks to stir.

700ml/24fl oz/scant 3 cups milk

250ml/8fl oz/1 cup espresso or very strong coffee

45ml/3 tbsp vanilla sugar, plus extra to taste

115g/4oz dark (bittersweet) chocolate, grated

Frothy Hot Chocolate

Real hot chocolate doesn't come as a powder in a packet – it is made with the best chocolate you can afford, whisked in hot milk until really frothy. This recipe uses dark (bittersweet) chocolate, but for a special treat you could use Mexican chocolate, which is flavoured with almonds, cinnamon and vanilla, and sweetened with sugar. All the ingredients are crushed together in a special mortar, and heated over coals. The powdered mixture is then shaped into discs, which can be bought in specialist stores.

SERVES FOUR

1 Pour the milk into a pan. Split the vanilla pod lengthways using a sharp knife to reveal the seeds, and add it to the milk; the vanilla seeds and the pod will flavour the milk.

2 Add the chocolate. The amount to use depends on personal taste – start with a smaller amount if you are unsure of the flavour and taste at the beginning of step 3, adding more if necessary.

3 Heat the chocolate milk gently, stirring until all the chocolate has melted and the mixture is smooth, then whisk with a wire whisk until the mixture boils. Remove the vanilla pod from the pan and divide the drink among four mugs or heatproof glasses. Serve the hot chocolate immediately.

1 litre/1¾ pints/ 4 cups milk

50–115g/2–4oz dark (bittersweet) chocolate, grated

1 vanilla pod (bean)

Appetizers
and Snacks

THE PERFECT APPETIZER OR SNACK TO SERVE WITH DRINKS

SHOULD LOOK FANTASTIC, TASTE DELICIOUS AND REQUIRE

THE MINIMUM OF EFFORT TO PREPARE. THE RECIPES IN THIS

CHAPTER DO JUST THAT, BRINGING TOGETHER DELICIOUS

COMBINATIONS OF FLAVOURS, TEXTURES, AROMAS AND

COLOURS TO WHET THE PALATE BEFORE THE MAIN COURSE.

Hummus

This classic Middle Eastern chickpea dip is flavoured with garlic and tahini (sesame seed paste). A little ground cumin can also be added, and olive oil can be stirred in to enrich the hummus, if you like. It is delicious served with wedges of toasted pitta bread or crudités.

SERVES FOUR TO SIX

1 Using a potato masher or fork, coarsely mash the chickpeas in a mixing bowl. If you like a smoother purée, process the chickpeas in a food processor or blender until a smooth paste is formed.

2 Mix the tahini into the bowl of chickpeas, then stir in the chopped garlic cloves and lemon juice. Season to taste with freshly ground black pepper and salt, and if needed, add a little water. Serve the hummus at room temperature.

400g/14oz can chickpeas, drained

60ml/4 tbsp tahini

2–3 garlic cloves, chopped

juice of ½–1 lemon

EXTRAS

Process 2 roasted red (bell) peppers with the chickpeas, then continue as above. Serve sprinkled with lightly toasted pine nuts and paprika mixed with olive oil.

Baba Ghanoush

Adjust the amount of aubergine, garlic and lemon juice in this richly flavoured Middle Eastern aubergine dip depending on how creamy, garlicky or tart you want it to be. The dip can served with a garnish of chopped fresh coriander leaves, olives or pickled cucumbers. Hot pepper sauce or a little ground coriander can be added, too.

SERVES TWO TO FOUR

1 large or 2 medium aubergines (eggplant)

2–4 garlic cloves, chopped

90–150ml/6–10 tbsp tahini

juice of 1 lemon, or to taste

1 Place the aubergine(s) directly over the flame of a gas stove or on the coals of a barbecue. Turn the aubergine(s) fairly frequently until deflated and the skin is evenly charred. Remove from the heat with tongs. Alternatively, place under a hot grill (broiler), turning frequently, until charred.

2 Put the aubergine(s) in a plastic bag and seal the top tightly, or place in a bowl and cover with crumpled kitchen paper. Leave to cool for 30–60 minutes.

3 Peel off the blackened skin from the aubergine(s), reserving the juices. Chop the aubergine flesh, either by hand for a coarse texture or in a food processor for a smooth purée. Put the aubergine in a bowl and stir in the reserved juices.

4 Add the garlic and tahini to the aubergine and stir until smooth. Stir in the lemon juice. If the mixture becomes too thick, add 15–30ml/1–2 tbsp water. Season with salt and ground black pepper to taste and spoon into a serving bowl. Serve at room temperature.

Mushroom Caviar

The name caviar refers to the dark colour and texture of this dish of chopped mushrooms. Serve the mushroom mixture in individual serving dishes with toasted rye bread rubbed with cut garlic cloves, to accompany. Chopped hard-boiled egg, spring onion and parsley, the traditional garnishes for caviar, can be added as a garnish.

SERVES FOUR

1 Heat the oil in a large pan, add the mushrooms, shallots and garlic, and cook, stirring occasionally, until browned. Season with salt, then continue cooking until the mushrooms give up their liquor.

2 Continue cooking, stirring frequently, until the liquor has evaporated and the mushrooms are brown and dry.

3 Put the mixture in a food processor or blender and process briefly until a chunky paste is formed. Spoon the mushroom caviar into dishes and serve.

45ml/3 tbsp olive or vegetable oil

450g/1lb mushrooms, coarsely chopped

5–10 shallots, chopped

4 garlic cloves, chopped

EXTRAS

For a rich wild mushroom caviar, soak 10–15g/¼–½oz dried porcini in about 120ml/4fl oz/ ½ cup water for about 30 minutes. Add the porcini and their soaking liquid to the browned mushrooms in step 2. Continue as in the recipe. Serve with wedges of lemon, for their tangy juice.

Brandade of Salt Cod

There are many versions of this creamy French salt cod purée: some contain mashed potatoes, others truffles. Serve the brandade with warmed crispbread or crusty bread for a tasty appetizer, or for a light lunch serve the brandade and bread with a tomato and basil salad. You can omit the garlic from the brandade, if you prefer, and serve toasted slices of French bread rubbed with garlic instead.

SERVES SIX

200g/7oz salt cod

250ml/8fl oz/1 cup extra virgin olive oil

4 garlic cloves, crushed

250ml/8fl oz/1 cup double (heavy) or whipping cream

1 Soak the fish in cold water for 24 hours, changing the water frequently. Drain the fish well. Cut the fish into pieces, place in a shallow pan and pour in enough cold water to cover. Heat the water until it is simmering and poach the fish for 8 minutes, until it is just cooked. Drain the fish, then remove the skin and bones.

2 Combine the extra virgin olive oil and crushed garlic cloves in a small pan and heat gently. In another pan, heat the double cream until it just starts to simmer.

3 Put the cod into a food processor, process it briefly, then gradually add alternate amounts of the garlic-flavoured olive oil and cream, while continuing to process the mixture. The aim is to create a purée with the consistency of mashed potato.

4 Season to taste with freshly ground black pepper, then scoop the brandade into a serving bowl or on to individual serving plates and serve with crispbread or crusty bread.

Chopped Egg and Onions

This dish is one of the oldest dishes in Jewish culinary history. It is delicious served sprinkled with chopped parsley and onion rings on crackers, piled on toast, or used as a sandwich or bagel filling. Serve chopped egg and onion as part of a buffet with a selection of dips and toppings.

SERVES FOUR TO SIX

1 Put the eggs in a large pan and cover with cold water. Bring the water to the boil and when it boils, reduce the heat and simmer over a low heat for 10 minutes.

2 Hold the boiled eggs under cold running water (if too hot to handle, place the eggs in a strainer and hold under the running water). When cool, remove the shells from the eggs and discard. Dry the eggs and chop coarsely.

3 Place the chopped eggs in a large bowl, add the onions, season generously with salt and black pepper and mix well. Add enough mayonnaise or chicken fat to bind the mixture together. Stir in the mustard, if using, and chill before serving.

8–10 eggs

6–8 spring onions (scallions) and/or 1 yellow or white onion, very finely chopped, plus extra to garnish

60–90ml/4–6 tbsp mayonnaise or rendered chicken fat

mild French wholegrain mustard, to taste (optional if using mayonnaise)

COOK'S TIP *The amount of rendered chicken fat or mayonnaise required will depend on how much onion you use in this dish.*

Israeli Cheese with Green Olives

In Israel, mild white cheeses spiked with seasonings, such as this one that is flavoured with piquant green olives, are served with drinks and little crackers or toast. It is also very good served for brunch – spread generously on chunks of fresh, crusty bread or bagels.

SERVES FOUR

175–200g/6–7oz soft white (farmer's) cheese

65g/2½oz feta cheese, preferably sheep's milk, lightly crumbled

20–30 pitted green olives, some chopped, the rest halved or quartered

2–3 large pinches of fresh thyme, plus extra to garnish

1 Place the soft white cheese in a mixing bowl and stir with the back of a spoon or a fork until soft and smooth. Add the crumbled feta cheese and stir the two cheeses together until they are thoroughly combined.

2 Add the chopped, halved and quartered olives and the pinches of fresh thyme to the cheese mixture and mix thoroughly.

3 Spoon the mixture into a bowl, sprinkle with thyme and serve with crackers, toast, chunks of bread or bagels.

Yogurt Cheese in Olive Oil

In Greece, sheep's yogurt is hung in muslin to drain off the whey before being patted into balls of soft cheese. Here the cheese is bottled in extra virgin olive oil with dried chillies and fresh herbs to make a wonderful gourmet gift or aromatic appetizer. It is delicious spread on thick slices of toast as a snack or a light lunch.

FILLS TWO 450G/1LB JARS

1 Sterilize a 30cm/12in square of muslin (cheesecloth) by soaking it in boiling water. Drain and lay it over a large plate. Season the yogurt generously with salt and tip on to the centre of the muslin. Bring up the sides of the muslin and tie firmly with string.

2 Hang the bag on a kitchen cupboard handle or suitable position where it can be suspended over a bowl to catch the whey. Leave for 2–3 days until the yogurt stops dripping.

3 Sterilize two 450g/1lb glass preserving or jam jars by heating them in the oven at 150°C/300°F/Gas 2 for 15 minutes.

4 Mix the crushed dried chillies and herbs. Take teaspoonfuls of the cheese and roll into balls with your hands. Lower into the jars, sprinkling each layer with the herb mixture.

5 Pour the oil over the cheese until completely covered. Store in the refrigerator for up to 3 weeks. To serve, spoon the cheese out of the jars with a little of the flavoured olive oil and spread on slices of lightly toasted bread.

1 litre/1¾ pints/ 4 cups Greek sheep's (US strained plain) yogurt

10ml/2 tsp crushed dried chillies or chilli powder

30ml/2 tbsp chopped fresh herbs, such as rosemary, and thyme or oregano

about 300ml/½ pint/ 1¼ cups extra virgin olive oil, preferably garlic-flavoured

Eggs Mimosa

Mimosa describes the fine yellow and white grated egg in this dish, which looks very similar to the flower of the same name. The eggs taste delicious when garnished with black pepper and basil leaves. Grated egg yolk can also be used as a garnish for a variety of other savoury dishes, such as sauces, soups and rice dishes.

MAKES TWENTY

1 Reserve two of the hard-boiled eggs and halve the remainder. Carefully remove the yolks with a teaspoon and blend them with the avocados, garlic and oil, adding freshly ground black pepper and salt to taste. Spoon or pipe the mixture into the halved egg whites using a piping (pastry) bag with a 1cm/½in or pipe star nozzle.

2 Sieve the remaining egg whites and sprinkle over the filled eggs. Sieve the yolks and arrange on top. Arrange the filled egg halves on a serving platter.

12 eggs, hard-boiled and peeled

2 ripe avocados, halved and stoned (pitted)

1 garlic clove, crushed

15ml/1 tbsp olive oil

> **COOK'S TIP**
> *You can prepare the mimosa garnish in advance and keep it in the refrigerator. Do not combine the egg white and yolk at this stage, but store in separate, airtight containers.*

Bacon-rolled Enokitake Mushrooms

The Japanese name for this dish is *Obimaki enoki*: an *obi* (belt or sash) is made from bacon and wrapped around enokitake mushrooms before they are grilled. The strong, smoky flavour of the bacon complements the subtle flavour of mushrooms. Small heaps of ground white pepper can be offered with these savouries, if you like.

SERVES FOUR

450g/1lb fresh enokitake mushrooms

6 rindless smoked streaky (fatty) bacon rashers (strips)

4 lemon wedges

1 Cut off the root part of each enokitake cluster 2cm/¾in from the end. Do not separate the stems. Cut the bacon rashers in half lengthways.

2 Divide the enokitake into 12 equal bunches. Take one bunch, then place the middle of the enokitake near the edge of one bacon rasher, with 2.5–4cm/1–1½in of enokitake protruding at each end.

3 Carefully roll up the bunch of enokitake in the bacon. Tuck any straying short stems into the bacon and slide the bacon slightly upwards at each roll to cover about 4cm/1½in of the enokitake. Secure the end of the bacon roll with a cocktail stick (toothpick). Repeat using the remaining enokitake and bacon to make 11 more rolls.

4 Preheat the grill (broiler) to high. Place the enokitake rolls on an oiled wire rack. Grill (broil) both sides until the bacon is crisp and the enokitake start to char. This takes 10–13 minutes.

5 Remove the enokitake rolls and place on a board. Using a fork and knife, chop each roll in half in the middle of the bacon belt. Arrange the top part of the enokitake roll standing upright, the bottom part lying down next to it. Add a wedge of lemon to each portion and serve.

Walnut and Goat's Cheese Bruschetta

The combination of toasted walnuts and melting goat's cheese is lovely in this simple appetizer, served with a pile of salad leaves. Toasting the walnuts helps to enhance their flavour. Walnut bread is readily available in most large supermarkets and makes an interesting alternative to ordinary crusty bread, although this can be used if walnut bread is unavailable.

SERVES FOUR

1 Preheat the grill (broiler). Lightly toast the walnut pieces, then remove and set aside. Put the walnut bread on a foil-lined grill rack and toast on one side. Turn the slices over and drizzle each with 15ml/1 tbsp of the French dressing.

2 Cut the goat's cheese into twelve slices and place three on each piece of bread. Grill (broil) for about 3 minutes, until the cheese is melting and beginning to brown.

3 Transfer the bruschetta to serving plates, sprinkle with the toasted walnuts and drizzle with the remaining French dressing. Serve the bruschetta immediately with salad leaves.

50g/2oz/½ cup walnut pieces

4 thick slices walnut bread

120ml/4fl oz/½ cup French dressing

200g/7oz chèvre or other semi-soft goat's cheese

COOK'S TIP *Use walnut bread slices from a slender loaf, so that the portions are not too wide. If you can buy only a large loaf, cut the slices in half to make neat, chunky pieces.*

Baked Eggs with Creamy Leeks

This simple but elegant appetizer is perfect for last-minute entertaining or quick dining. Garnish the baked eggs with crisp, fried fresh sage leaves and serve with warm, fresh crusty bread for a special meal. Small- to medium-sized leeks (less than 2.5cm/1in in diameter) are best for this dish as they have the most tender flavour and only require a short cooking time.

SERVES FOUR

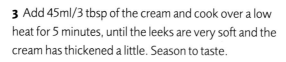

1 Preheat the oven to 190°C/375°F/Gas 5. Generously butter the base and sides of four ramekins.

2 Melt the butter in a frying pan and cook the leeks over a medium heat, stirring frequently, for 3–5 minutes, until softened and translucent, but not browned.

3 Add 45ml/3 tbsp of the cream and cook over a low heat for 5 minutes, until the leeks are very soft and the cream has thickened a little. Season to taste.

4 Place the ramekins in a small roasting pan and divide the leeks among them. Break an egg into each, spoon over the remaining cream and season.

5 Pour boiling water into the roasting pan to come about halfway up the sides of the ramekins. Transfer the pan to the oven and bake in the preheated oven for about 10 minutes, until just set. Serve piping hot.

15g/½oz/1 tbsp butter, plus extra for greasing

225g/8oz small leeks, thinly sliced

75–90ml/5–6 tbsp whipping cream

4 small–medium (US medium–large) eggs

COOK'S TIP *For a slightly different result, beat the eggs with the remaining whipping cream and seasoning in step 4 and spoon over the leeks, then bake in the roasting pan as for step 5.*

Red Onion and Olive Pissaladière

For a taste of the Mediterranean, try this French-style pizza – it makes a delicious and easy snack. Cook the sliced red onions slowly until they are caramelized and sweet before piling them into the pastry cases. To prepare the recipe in advance, pile the cooled onions on to the pastry round and chill the pissaladière until you are ready to bake it.

SERVES SIX

1 Preheat the oven to 220°C/425°F/Gas 7. Heat the oil in a large, heavy frying pan and cook the onions gently, stirring frequently, for 15–20 minutes, until they are soft and golden. Season to taste.

2 Roll out the pastry thinly on a floured surface. Cut out a 33cm/13in round and transfer it to a lightly dampened baking sheet.

3 Spread the onions over the pastry in an even layer to within 1cm/½in of the edge. Sprinkle the olives on top. Bake the tart for 20–25 minutes, until the pastry is risen and deep golden. Cut into wedges and serve warm.

75ml/5 tbsp extra virgin olive oil

500g/1¼lb small red onions, thinly sliced

500g/1¼lb puff pastry, thawed if frozen

75g/3oz/¾ cup small pitted black olives

Figs with Prosciutto and Roquefort

Fresh figs are a delicious treat, whether you choose dark purple, yellowy green or green-skinned varieties. When they are ripe, you can split them open with your fingers to reveal the soft, sweet flesh full of edible seeds. In this easy, stylish dish figs and honey balance the richness of the ham and cheese. Serve with warm bread for a simple appetizer before any rich main course.

SERVES FOUR

1 Preheat the grill (broiler). Quarter the figs and place on a foil-lined grill rack. Tear each slice of prosciutto into two or three pieces and crumple them up on the foil beside the figs. Brush the figs with 15ml/1 tbsp of the clear honey and cook under the grill until lightly browned.

2 Crumble the Roquefort cheese and divide among four plates, setting it to one side. Add the honey-grilled figs and ham and pour over any cooking juices caught on the foil. Drizzle the remaining honey over the figs, ham and cheese, and serve seasoned with plenty of freshly ground black pepper.

8 fresh figs

75g/3oz prosciutto

45ml/3 tbsp clear honey

75g/3oz Roquefort cheese

Crisp Fried Whitebait

This must be one of the simplest of all classic fish dishes and it is absolutely delicious with lemon wedges and thinly sliced brown bread and butter. If you prefer, serve the whitebait with a simple lemon and herb dip – mix 150ml/¼ pint/⅔ cup natural (plain) yogurt with the rind of one lemon and 45ml/ 3 tbsp chopped fresh herbs. Serve chilled.

SERVES FOUR

oil, for deep-frying

150ml/¼ pint/⅔ cup milk

115g/4oz/1 cup plain (all-purpose) flour

450g/1lb whitebait

<table>
<tr><td rowspan="2">C O O K ' S   T I P</td><td>Most whitebait are sold frozen. Thaw them before use and dry them thoroughly on kitchen paper before flouring.</td></tr>
</table>

1 Heat the oil in a large pan or deep-fryer. Put the milk in a shallow bowl and spoon the flour into a paper bag. Season the flour well with salt and pepper.

2 Dip a handful of the whitebait into the bowl of milk, drain them well, then pop them into the paper bag. Shake gently to coat them evenly in the seasoned flour, then transfer to a plate. Repeat until all the fish have been coated. This is the easiest method of flouring whitebait before frying, but don't add too many at once to the bag, or they will stick together.

3 Heat the oil for deep-frying to 190°C/375°F or until a cube of stale bread, dropped into the oil, browns in about 20 seconds. Add a batch of whitebait, preferably in a frying basket, and deep-fry for 2–3 minutes, until crisp and golden brown. Drain and keep hot while you cook the rest. Serve very hot.

Soups

SOUP IS ONE OF THE MOST VERSATILE DISHES AROUND AND
CAN BE SERVED AS AN ELEGANT APPETIZER OR A WARMING
MEAL. FROM CHILLED SUMMER SOUPS TO WARMING
WINTER BROTHS, THEY ARE INCREDIBLY EASY TO MAKE AND
ONLY NEED A FEW INGREDIENTS AND FLAVOURINGS TO
CREATE FABULOUS, MOUTHWATERING RESULTS.

Avocado Soup

This delicious soup has a fresh, delicate flavour and a wonderful colour. For added zest, add a generous squeeze of lime juice or spoon 15ml/1 tbsp salsa into the soup just before serving. Choose ripe avocados for this soup – they should feel soft when gently pressed. Keep very firm avocados at room temperature for 3–4 days until they soften. To speed ripening, place in a brown paper bag.

SERVES FOUR

1 Cut the avocados in half, remove the peel and lift out the stones (pits). Chop the flesh coarsely and place it in a food processor with 45–60ml/3–4 tbsp of the sour cream. Process until smooth.

2 Heat the chicken stock in a pan. When it is hot, but still below simmering point, stir in the rest of the cream with salt to taste.

3 Gradually stir the avocado mixture into the hot stock. Heat gently but do not let the mixture approach boiling point.

4 Chop the coriander. Ladle the soup into individual heated bowls and sprinkle each portion with chopped coriander and black pepper. Serve immediately.

2 large ripe avocados

300ml/½ pint/1¼ cups sour cream

1 litre/1¾ pints/ 4 cups well-flavoured chicken stock

small bunch of fresh coriander (cilantro)

Vichyssoise

This classic, chilled summer soup of leeks and potatoes was first created in the 1920s by Louis Diat, chef at the New York Ritz-Carlton. He named it after Vichy near his home in France. The soup can be sharpened with lemon juice, enriched with swirls of cream and garnished with chives.

SERVES FOUR TO SIX

50g/2oz/¼ cup unsalted (sweet) butter

600g/1lb 5oz leeks, white parts only, thinly sliced

250g/9oz floury potatoes (such as King Edward or Maris Piper), peeled and cut into chunks

1.5 litres/2½ pints/6½ cups half and half light chicken stock or water and milk

1 Melt the unsalted butter in a heavy pan and cook the leeks, covered, for 15–20 minutes, until they are soft but not browned.

2 Add the potato chunks and cook over a low heat, uncovered, for a few minutes.

3 Stir in the stock or water and milk, with salt and pepper to taste. Bring to the boil, then reduce the heat and partly cover the pan. Simmer for 15 minutes, or until the potatoes are soft.

4 Cool, then process the soup until smooth in a blender or food processor. Sieve the soup into a bowl. Taste and adjust the seasoning and add a little iced water if the consistency of the soup seems too thick.

5 Chill the soup for at least 4 hours or until very cold. Taste the chilled soup for seasoning again before serving. Pour the soup into bowls and serve.

EXTRAS *To make a fabulous chilled leek and sorrel or watercress soup, add about 50g/2oz/1 cup shredded sorrel to the soup at the end of cooking. Finish and chill as in the main recipe, then serve the soup garnished with a little pile of finely shredded sorrel. The same quantity of watercress can also be used.*

Avgolemono

The name of this popular Greek soup means egg and lemon, the two essential ingredients that produce a light, nourishing soup. The soup also contains orzo, which is Greek, rice-shaped pasta, but you can use any small shape. Serve the soup with thin slices of lightly toasted bread and add a garnish of very thin lemon slices for a pretty appearance on special occasions.

SERVES FOUR TO SIX

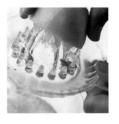

1 Pour the chicken stock into a large pan and bring to the boil. Add the orzo pasta or other small pasta shapes and cook for 5 minutes, or according to the packet instructions.

2 Beat the eggs until they are frothy, then add the lemon juice and a tablespoon of cold water. Slowly stir in a ladleful of the hot chicken stock, then add one or two more. Remove the pan from the heat, then pour in the egg mixture and stir well. Season to taste with salt and freshly ground black pepper and serve immediately. (Do not let the soup boil once the egg, lemon juice and stock mixture has been added, or it will curdle.)

1.75 litres/3 pints/ 7½ cups chicken stock

115g/4oz/½ cup orzo pasta

3 eggs

juice of 1 large lemon

Simple Cream of Onion Soup

This wonderfully soothing soup has a deep, buttery flavour that is achieved with only a few ingredients and the minimum of fuss. It makes delicious comfort food on a cold day. Use home-made stock if you have it, or buy fresh stock for the best flavour. Crisp croûtons or chopped chives complement the smooth soup when sprinkled over just before serving.

SERVES FOUR

**115g/4oz/
½ cup unsalted
(sweet) butter**

**1kg/2¼lb yellow
onions, sliced**

**1 litre/1¾ pints/4 cups
good chicken or
vegetable stock**

**150ml/¼ pint/⅔ cup
double (heavy) cream**

1 Melt 75g/3oz/6 tbsp of the unsalted butter in a large, heavy pan. Set about 200g/7oz of the onions aside and add the rest to the pan. Stir to coat in the butter, then cover and cook very gently for about 30 minutes. The onions should be very soft and tender, but not browned.

2 Add the chicken or vegetable stock, 5ml/1 tsp salt and freshly ground black pepper to taste. Bring to the boil, reduce the heat and simmer for 5 minutes, then remove from the heat.

3 Leave the soup to cool, then process it in a blender or food processor. Return the soup to the rinsed pan.

4 Meanwhile, melt the remaining butter in another pan and cook the remaining onions over a low heat, covered, until soft but not browned. Uncover and continue to cook the onions gently until they turn golden yellow.

5 Add the cream to the soup and reheat it gently until hot, but do not allow it to boil. Taste and adjust the seasoning. Add the buttery onions and stir for 1–2 minutes, then ladle the soup into bowls. Serve the soup immediately.

COOK'S TIP

Adding the second batch of onions gives texture and a lovely buttery flavour to this soup. Make sure the onions do not brown or crisp.

Cappelletti in Broth

This soup is traditionally served in northern Italy on Santo Stefano (St Stephen's Day, the day after Christmas) and on New Year's Day as a welcome light change from all the special celebration food. Cappelletti are little stuffed pasta shapes that resemble hats.

SERVES FOUR

1 Pour the chicken stock into a large pan and bring to the boil. Add a little seasoning to taste, then drop in the pasta.

2 Stir well and bring back to the boil. Lower the heat to a simmer and cook according to the instructions on the packet, until the pasta is *al dente*, that is, tender but still firm to the bite.

3 Swirl in the finely chopped fresh flat leaf parsley, if using, then taste and adjust the seasoning, if necessary. Ladle into four warmed soup plates, then sprinkle with the freshly grated Parmesan cheese and serve immediately.

1.2 litres/2 pints/ 5 cups chicken stock

90–115g/3½–4oz/ 1 cup fresh or dried cappelletti

about 45ml/3 tbsp finely chopped fresh flat leaf parsley (optional)

about 30ml/2 tbsp freshly grated Parmesan cheese

COOK'S TIP *If you don't have home-made stock use two 300g/11oz cans of condensed beef consommé, adding water as instructed, or chilled commercial stock.*

Tiny Pasta in Broth

This Italian soup is ideal for a light supper served with ciabatta bread and also makes a delicious first course for an *al fresco* supper. A wide variety of different types of *pastina* or soup pasta are available including stellette (stars), anellini (tiny thin rounds), risoni (rice-shaped) and farfalline (little butterflies). Choose just one shape or a combination of different varieties for an interesting result.

SERVES FOUR

1.2 litres/2 pints/ 5 cups beef stock

75g/3oz/¾ cup dried tiny soup pasta

2 pieces bottled roasted red (bell) pepper, about 50g/2oz

coarsely shaved Parmesan cheese

1 Bring the beef stock to the boil in a large pan. Add seasoning to taste, then drop in the dried soup pasta. Stir well and bring the stock back to the boil.

2 Reduce the heat so that the soup simmers and cook for 7–8 minutes, or according to the packet instructions, until the pasta is *al dente*, that is, tender but still firm to the bite.

3 Drain the pieces of roasted pepper and dice them finely. Place them in the base of four warmed soup plates. Taste the soup for seasoning before ladling it into the soup plates. Serve immediately, topped with shavings of Parmesan.

Potato and Roasted Garlic Broth

Roasted garlic takes on a mellow, sweet flavour that is subtle, not overpowering, in this delicious vegetarian soup. Choose floury potatoes for this soup, such as Maris Piper, Estima, Cara or King Edward – they will give the soup a delicious velvety texture. Serve the broth piping hot with melted Cheddar or Gruyère cheese on French bread, as the perfect winter warmer.

SERVES FOUR

1 Preheat the oven to 190°C/375°F/Gas 5. Place the unpeeled garlic bulbs or bulb in a small roasting pan and bake for 30 minutes until soft in the centre.

2 Meanwhile, par-boil the potatoes in a large pan of lightly salted boiling water for 10 minutes.

3 Simmer the stock in another pan for 5 minutes. Drain the potatoes and add them to the stock.

4 Squeeze the garlic pulp into the soup, reserving a few whole cloves, stir and season to taste. Simmer for 15 minutes and serve topped with whole garlic cloves and parsley.

2 small or 1 large whole head of garlic (about 20 cloves)

4 medium potatoes (about 500g/1¼lb in total), diced

1.75 litres/3 pints/ 7½ cups good-quality hot vegetable stock

chopped flat leaf parsley, to garnish

Winter Squash Soup with Tomato Salsa

Creamy butternut squash makes good soup with very few additional ingredients. Select a really good bought salsa for this soup and add a sprinkling of chopped fresh oregano or marjoram as a garnish.

SERVES FOUR TO FIVE

1 large butternut squash or small pumpkin, halved and seeded

75ml/5 tbsp garlic-flavoured olive oil

2 onions, chopped

60–120ml/4–8 tbsp tomato salsa

1 Preheat the oven to 220°C/425°F/Gas 7. Place the butternut squash or pumpkin on a baking sheet and brush with some of the oil and roast for 25 minutes. Reduce the temperature to 190°C/375°F/Gas 5 and cook for 20–25 minutes more, or until the squash is tender.

2 Heat the remaining oil in a large, heavy pan and cook the chopped onions over a low heat for about 10 minutes, or until softened.

3 Meanwhile, scoop the squash out of its skin, adding it to the pan. Pour in 1.2 litres/2 pints/5 cups water and stir in 5ml/1 tsp salt and plenty of black pepper. Bring to the boil, cover and simmer for 10 minutes.

4 Cool the soup slightly, then process it in a blender or food processor to a smooth purée. Alternatively, press the soup through a fine sieve with the back of a spoon. Reheat without boiling, then ladle it into warmed bowls. Top each serving with a spoonfuls of salsa and serve.

Butter Bean, Sun-dried Tomato and Pesto Soup

This soup is so quick and easy to make: the key is to use a good-quality home-made or bought fresh stock for the best result. Using plenty of pesto and sun-dried tomato purée (paste) gives it a rich, minestrone-like flavour. As an alternative to butter beans, haricot (navy) or cannellini beans will make good substitutes.

SERVES FOUR

1 Put the stock in a pan with the butter beans and bring just to the boil. Reduce the heat and stir in the tomato purée and pesto. Cook gently for 5 minutes.

2 Transfer six ladlefuls of the soup to a blender or food processor, scooping up plenty of the beans. Process until smooth, then return the purée to the pan.

3 Heat gently, stirring frequently, for 5 minutes, then season if necessary. Ladle into four warmed soup bowls and serve with warm crusty bread or breadsticks.

900ml/1½ pints/ 3¾ cups chicken or vegetable stock

2 x 400g/14oz cans butter (lima) beans, drained and rinsed

60ml/4 tbsp sun-dried tomato purée (paste)

75ml/5 tbsp pesto

Stilton and Watercress Soup

A good creamy Stilton and plenty of peppery watercress bring maximum flavour to this rich, smooth soup, which is superlative in small portions. Rocket (arugula) can be used as an alternative to watercress – both leaves are an excellent source of iron. When choosing any salad leaves, look for crisp, fresh leaves and reject any wilted or discoloured greens.

SERVES FOUR TO SIX

1 Pour the stock into a pan and bring almost to the boil. Remove and discard any very large stalks from the watercress. Add the watercress to the pan and simmer gently for 2–3 minutes, until tender.

2 Crumble the cheese into the pan and simmer for 1 minute more, until the cheese has started to melt. Process the soup in a blender or food processor, in batches if necessary, until very smooth. Return the soup to the pan.

3 Stir in the cream and check the seasoning. The soup will probably not need any extra salt, as the blue cheese is already quite salty. Heat the soup gently, without boiling, then ladle it into warm bowls.

600ml/1 pint/ 2½ cups chicken or vegetable stock

225g/8oz watercress

150g/5oz Stilton or other blue cheese

150ml/¼ pint/⅔ cup single (light) cream

Fish and Shellfish

THE DELICATE TASTE OF FISH AND SHELLFISH IS PERFECTLY

SUITED TO SUBTLE, SIMPLE FLAVOURINGS SUCH AS FRESH

HERBS, CITRUS JUICE, SUCCULENT TOMATOES OR SMOKY

BACON. THE FABULOUS RECIPES IN THIS CHAPTER MAKE

THE MOST OF SIMPLE, SEASONAL INGREDIENTS TO ACHIEVE

TRULY WONDERFUL DISHES.

Sea Bass in a Salt Crust

Baking fish in a crust of sea salt seals in and enhances its flavour. Any firm fish can be cooked in this way. Decorate with a garnish of seaweed or blanched samphire and lemon slices, and break open the crust at the table to release the glorious aroma. Serve the fish with baby new potatoes roasted with olive oil and a sprinkling of dried rosemary, and steamed green vegetables such as broccoli or green beans.

SERVES FOUR

1 Preheat the oven to 240°C/475°F/Gas 9. Fill the cavity of the fish with the sprigs of fresh fennel, rosemary and thyme, and grind over some of the mixed peppercorns.

2 Spread half the salt in an ovenproof dish (ideally oval) and lay the sea bass on it. Cover the fish all over with a 1cm/½in layer of salt, pressing it down firmly. Moisten the salt lightly by spraying with water from an atomizer. Bake the fish for 30–40 minutes, until the salt crust is just beginning to colour.

3 Bring the sea bass to the table in its salt crust. Use a sharp knife to break open the crust and cut into four portions.

1 sea bass, about 1kg/2¼lb, cleaned and scaled

1 sprig each of fresh fennel, rosemary and thyme

mixed peppercorns

2kg/4½lb coarse sea salt

Roast Cod Wrapped in Prosciutto with Vine Tomatoes

Wrapping chunky fillets of cod in wafer-thin slices of prosciutto keeps the fish succulent and moist, at the same time adding flavour and visual impact. Serve with baby new potatoes and a herb salad for a stylish supper or lunch dish.

SERVES FOUR

1 Preheat the oven to 220°C/425°F/Gas 7. Pat the fish dry on kitchen paper and remove any stray bones. Season lightly on both sides with salt and pepper.

2 Place one fillet in an ovenproof dish and drizzle 15ml/1 tbsp of the oil over it. Cover with the second fillet, laying the thick end on top of the thin end of the lower fillet to create an even shape. Lay the ham over the fish, overlapping the slices to cover the fish in an even layer. Tuck the ends of the ham under the fish and tie it in place at intervals with fine string.

3 Using kitchen scissors, snip the tomato vines into four portions and add to the dish. Drizzle the tomatoes and ham with the remaining oil and season lightly. Roast for about 35 minutes, until the tomatoes are tender and lightly coloured and the fish is cooked through. Test the fish by piercing one end of the parcel with the tip of a sharp knife to check that it flakes easily.

4 Slice the fish and transfer the portions to warm plates, adding the tomatoes. Spoon over the cooking juices from the dish and serve immediately.

2 thick skinless cod fillets, each weighing about 375g/13oz

75ml/5 tbsp extra virgin olive oil

75g/3oz prosciutto, thinly sliced

400g/14oz tomatoes, on the vine

Tonno con Piselli

This Jewish Italian dish of fresh tuna and peas is especially enjoyed at Passover, which falls in spring. Before the days of the freezer, little peas were only eaten at this time of year when they were in season. At other times of the year chickpeas were used instead – they give a heartier result.

SERVES FOUR

1 Preheat the oven to 190°C/375°F/Gas 5. Sprinkle the tuna steaks on each side with salt and plenty of freshly ground black pepper and place in a shallow ovenproof dish, in a single layer.

2 Bring the tomato sauce to the boil, then add the fresh shelled or frozen peas and chopped fresh flat leaf parsley. Pour the sauce and peas evenly over the fish steaks in the ovenproof dish and bake in the preheated oven, uncovered, for about 20 minutes, or until the fish is tender. Serve the fish, sauce and peas immediately, straight from the dish.

350g/12oz tuna steaks

600ml/1 pint/2½ cups fresh tomato sauce

350g/12oz/3 cups fresh shelled or frozen peas

45ml/3 tbsp chopped fresh flat leaf parsley

VARIATION This recipe works well with other types and cuts of fish. Use tuna fillets in place of the steaks or try different fish steaks, such as salmon or swordfish.

Filo-wrapped Fish

Select a chunky variety of tomato sauce for this simple but delicious recipe. The choice of fish can be varied according to what is in season and what is freshest on the day of purchase. When working with filo pastry, keep it covered with clear film (plastic wrap) or a damp dishtowel, as once it's exposed to air it dries out quickly and is difficult to handle.

SERVES THREE TO FOUR

**about 130g/4½oz
filo pastry
(6–8 large sheets)**

**about 30ml/2 tbsp
olive oil, for brushing**

**450g/1lb salmon or cod
steaks or fillets**

**550ml/18fl oz/2½ cups
fresh tomato sauce**

1 Preheat the oven to 200°C/400°F/Gas 6. Take a sheet of filo pastry, brush with a little olive oil and cover with a second sheet of pastry. Place a piece of fish on top of the pastry, towards the bottom edge, then top with 1–2 spoonfuls of the tomato sauce, spreading it in an even layer.

2 Roll the fish in the pastry, taking care to enclose the filling completely. Brush with a little olive oil. Arrange on a baking sheet and repeat with the remaining fish and pastry. You should have about half the sauce remaining, to serve with the fish.

3 Bake for 10–15 minutes, or until golden. Meanwhile, reheat the remaining sauce. Serve immediately with the remaining sauce.

Poached Fish in Spicy Tomato Sauce

A selection of white fish fillets are used in this Middle-Eastern dish – cod, haddock, hake or halibut are all good. Serve the fish with flat breads, such as pitta, and a spicy tomato relish. It is also good with couscous or rice and a green salad with a refreshing lemon juice dressing.

SERVES EIGHT

1 Heat the tomato sauce with the harissa and coriander in a large pan. Add seasoning to taste and bring to the boil.

2 Remove the pan from the heat and add the fish to the hot sauce. Return to the heat and bring the sauce to the boil again. Reduce the heat and simmer very gently for about 5 minutes, or until the fish is tender. (Test with a fork: if the flesh flakes easily, then it is cooked.)

3 Taste the sauce and adjust the seasoning, adding more harissa if necessary. Serve hot or warm.

600ml/1 pint/2½ cups fresh tomato sauce

2.5–5ml/½–1 tsp harissa

60ml/4 tbsp chopped fresh coriander (cilantro) leaves

1.5kg/3¼lb mixed white fish fillets, cut into chunks

COOK'S TIP *Harissa is a chilli paste spiced with cumin, garlic and coriander. It is fiery and should be used with care until you are familiar with the flavour. Start by adding a small amount and then add more after tasting the sauce.*

Fish with Tomato and Pine Nuts

Whole fish marinated in lemon juice and cooked with pine nuts in a spicy tomato sauce is a speciality of Jewish cooking, particularly as a festival treat for Rosh Hashanah, the Jewish New Year. The fish may be cooked and served with head and tail on, as here, or if you like, with these removed. A simple garnish of flat leaf parsley improves the appearance of this delicious dish.

SERVES SIX TO EIGHT

1–1.5kg/2¼–3¼lb fish, such as snapper, cleaned, with head and tail left on

juice of 2 lemons

65g/2½oz/scant ¾ cup pine nuts, toasted

350ml/12fl oz/1½ cups spicy tomato sauce

1 Prick the fish all over with a fork and rub with 2.5ml/½ tsp salt. Put the fish in a roasting pan or large dish and pour over the lemon juice. Leave to stand for 2 hours.

2 Preheat the oven to 180°C/350°F/Gas 4. Sprinkle half of the pine nuts over the base of an ovenproof dish, top with half of the sauce, then add the fish and its marinade. Add the remaining tomato sauce and the remaining pine nuts.

3 Cover the ovenproof dish tightly with a lid or foil and bake in the preheated oven for 30 minutes, or until the fish is tender. Serve the fish immediately, straight from the dish.

Baked Salmon with Green Sauce

When buying whole salmon, there are several points to consider – the skin should be bright and shiny, the eyes should be bright and the tail should look fresh and moist. Baking the salmon in foil produces a moist result, rather like poaching, but with the ease of baking. Garnish the fish with thin slices of cucumber and dill to conceal any flesh that may look ragged after skinning and serve with lemon wedges.

SERVES SIX TO EIGHT

2–3kg/4½–6¾lb salmon, cleaned with head and tail left on

3–5 spring onions (scallions), thinly sliced

1 lemon, thinly sliced

600ml/1 pint/2½ cups watercress sauce or herb mayonnaise

1 Preheat the oven to 180°C/350°F/Gas 4. Rinse the salmon and lay it on a large piece of foil. Stuff the fish with the sliced spring onions and layer the lemon slices inside and around the fish, then sprinkle with plenty of salt and ground black pepper.

2 Loosely fold the foil around the fish and fold the edges over to seal. Bake for about 1 hour.

3 Remove the fish from the oven and leave to stand, still wrapped in the foil, for about 15 minutes, then unwrap the parcel and leave the fish to cool.

4 When the fish is cool, carefully lift it on to a large plate, retaining the lemon slices. Cover the fish tightly with clear film (plastic wrap) and chill for several hours.

5 Before serving, discard the lemon slices from around the fish. Using a blunt knife to lift up the edge of the skin, carefully peel the skin away from the flesh, avoiding tearing the flesh, and pull out any fins at the same time.

6 Chill the watercress sauce or herb mayonnaise before serving. Transfer the fish to a serving platter and serve the sauce separately.

VARIATION

Instead of cooking a whole fish, prepare 6–8 salmon steaks. Place each fish steak on an individual square of foil, then top with a slice of onion and a slice of lemon and season generously with salt and ground black pepper. Loosely wrap the foil up around the fish, fold the edges to seal and place the parcels on a baking sheet. Bake the steaks for 10–15 minutes, or until the flesh is opaque. Serve the fish cold with the chilled watercress sauce or herb mayonnaise.

Haddock with Fennel Butter

Fresh fish tastes fabulous cooked in a simple herb butter. Here the liquorice flavour of fennel complements the haddock beautifully to make a simple dish ideal for a dinner party. If you can buy only small haddock fillets, fold them in half before baking, or use cod as an alternative. Serve tiny new potatoes and a herb salad with the fish to make a light, summery main course.

SERVES FOUR

1 Preheat the oven to 220°C/425°F/Gas 7. Season the fish on both sides with salt and pepper. Melt one-quarter of the butter in a frying pan, preferably non-stick, and cook the fish over a medium heat briefly on both sides.

2 Transfer the fish to a shallow ovenproof dish. Cut four wafer-thin slices from the lemon and squeeze the juice from the remainder over the fish. Place the lemon slices on top and then bake for 15–20 minutes, or until the fish is cooked.

3 Meanwhile, melt the remaining butter in the frying pan and add the fennel and a little seasoning.

4 Transfer the cooked fish to plates and pour the cooking juices into the herb butter. Heat gently for a few seconds, then pour the herb butter over the fish. Serve immediately.

675g/1½lb haddock fillet, skinned and cut into 4 portions

50g/2oz/¼ cup butter

1 lemon

45ml/3 tbsp coarsely chopped fennel

Crab and Cucumber Wraps

This dish is a modern twist on the ever-popular Chinese classic, crispy Peking duck with pancakes. In this quick and easy version, crisp, refreshing cucumber and full-flavoured dressed crab are delicious with spicy-sweet hoisin sauce in warm tortilla wraps. Serve the wraps as an appetizer for four people, or as a main course for two.

SERVES TWO

1 Cut the cucumber into small even-sized batons. Scoop the dressed crab into a small mixing bowl, add a little freshly ground black pepper and mix lightly to combine.

2 Heat the tortillas gently, one at a time, in a heavy frying pan until they begin to colour on each side.

3 Spread a tortilla with 30ml/2 tbsp hoisin sauce, then sprinkle with one-quarter of the cucumber. Arrange one-quarter of the seasoned crab meat down the centre of each tortilla and roll up. Repeat with the remaining ingredients. Serve immediately.

½ cucumber

1 medium dressed crab

4 small wheat tortillas

120ml/8 tbsp hoisin sauce

Scallops with Fennel and Bacon

This dish is a delicious combination of succulent scallops and crispy bacon, served on a bed of tender fennel and melting mascarpone. If you can't get large scallops (known as king scallops), buy the smaller queen scallops and serve a dozen per person. If you buy scallops in the shell, wash and keep the pretty fan-shaped shells to serve a range of fish dishes in.

SERVES TWO

1 Trim, halve and slice the fennel, reserving and chopping any feathery tops. Blanch the slices in boiling water for about 3 minutes, until softened, then drain.

2 Preheat the grill (broiler) to moderate. Place the fennel in a shallow flameproof dish and season with salt and pepper. Dot with the mascarpone and grill (broil) for about 5 minutes, until the cheese has melted and the fennel is lightly browned.

3 Meanwhile, pat the scallops dry on kitchen paper and season lightly. Cook the bacon in a large, heavy frying pan, until crisp and golden, turning once. Drain and keep warm. Fry the scallops in the bacon fat for 1–2 minutes on each side, until cooked through.

4 Transfer the fennel to serving plates and crumble or snip the bacon into bite size pieces over the top. Pile the scallops on the bacon and sprinkle with any reserved fennel tops.

2 small fennel bulbs

130g/4½oz/ generous ½ cup mascarpone cheese

8 large scallops, shelled

75g/3oz thin smoked streaky (fatty) bacon rashers (strips)

Prawn and New Potato Stew

New potatoes with plenty of flavour, such as Jersey Royals, Maris Piper or Nicola, are essential for this effortless stew. Use a good quality jar of tomato and chilli sauce; there are now plenty available in the supermarkets. For a really easy supper dish, serve with warm, crusty bread to mop up the delicious sauce, and a mixed green salad.

SERVES FOUR

675g/1½lb small new potatoes, scrubbed

15g/½oz/½ cup fresh coriander (cilantro)

350g/12oz jar tomato and chilli sauce

300g/11oz cooked peeled prawns (shrimp), thawed and drained if frozen

1 Cook the potatoes in lightly salted, boiling water for 15 minutes, until tender. Drain and return to the pan.

2 Finely chop half the coriander and add to the pan with the tomato and chilli sauce and 90ml/6 tbsp water. Bring to the boil, reduce the heat, cover and simmer gently for 5 minutes.

3 Stir in the prawns and heat briefly until they are warmed through. Do not overheat the prawns or they will quickly shrivel, becoming tough and tasteless. Spoon into shallow bowls and serve sprinkled with the remaining coriander, torn into pieces.

Meat and Poultry

WITH THE SIMPLE ADDITION OF A FEW WELL-CHOSEN
INGREDIENTS, MEAT AND POULTRY CAN BE TRANSFORMED
INTO EXCITING, INNOVATIVE DISHES. FROM STEAK TO DUCK
AND FROM PORK TO PHEASANT, THIS CHAPTER INCLUDES A
WONDERFUL SELECTION OF DISHES THAT ARE EQUALLY
SUITED TO A QUICK FAMILY SUPPER OR A DINNER PARTY.

Beef Patties with Onions and Peppers

This is a firm family favourite. It is easy to make and delicious, and it can be varied by adding other vegetables, such as sliced red peppers, broccoli or mushrooms. These patties are very versatile and can be served in a variety of ways – with chunky home-made chips (fries), with crusty bread, or with rice and a ready-made tomato sauce.

SERVES FOUR

1 Place the minced beef, chopped onion and 15ml/1 tbsp garlic-flavoured oil in a bowl and mix well. Season well and form into four large or eight small patties.

2 Heat the remaining oil in a large non-stick pan, then add the patties and cook on both sides until browned. Sprinkle over 15ml/1 tbsp water and add a little seasoning.

3 Cover the patties with the sliced onions and peppers. Sprinkle in another 15ml/1 tbsp water and a little seasoning, then cover the pan. Reduce the heat to very low and braise for 20–30 minutes.

4 When the onions are turning golden brown, remove the pan from the heat. Serve the patties with onions and peppers.

500g/1¼lb lean minced (ground) beef

4 onions, 1 finely chopped and 3 sliced

30ml/2 tbsp garlic-flavoured olive oil or olive oil

2–3 green (bell) peppers, seeded and sliced lengthways into strips

Steak with Warm Tomato Salsa

A refreshing, tangy salsa of tomatoes, spring onions and balsamic vinegar makes a colourful topping for chunky, pan-fried steaks. Choose rump, sirloin or fillet – whichever is your favourite – and if you do not have a non-stick pan, grill the steak instead for the same length of time. Serve with potato wedges and a mixed leaf salad with a mustard dressing.

SERVES TWO

1 Trim any excess fat from the steaks, then season on both sides with salt and pepper. Heat a non-stick frying pan and cook the steaks for about 3 minutes on each side for medium rare. Cook for a little longer if you like your steak well cooked.

2 Meanwhile, put the tomatoes in a heatproof bowl, cover with boiling water and leave for 1–2 minutes, until the skins start to split. Drain and peel the tomatoes, then halve them and scoop out the seeds. Dice the tomato flesh. Thinly slice the spring onions.

3 Transfer the steaks to plates and keep warm. Add the vegetables, balsamic vinegar, 30ml/2 tbsp water and a little seasoning to the cooking juices in the pan and stir briefly until warm, scraping up any meat residue. Spoon the salsa over the steaks to serve.

2 steaks, about 2cm/ ¾ in thick

4 large plum tomatoes

2 spring onions (scallions)

30ml/2 tbsp balsamic vinegar

North African Lamb

This dish is full of contrasting flavours that create a rich, spicy and fruity main course. For best results, use lamb that still retains some fat, as this will help keep the meat moist and succulent during roasting. Serve the lamb with couscous or mixed white and wild rice, sprinkled with chopped coriander (cilantro). Roasted chunks of red and yellow (bell) peppers, aubergine (eggplant) and courgettes (zucchini), cooked in the oven with the lamb, complete the meal.

SERVES FOUR

1 Preheat the oven to 200°C/400°F/Gas 6. Season the lamb with salt and pepper. Heat a frying pan, preferably non-stick, and cook the lamb on all sides until beginning to brown. Transfer to a roasting pan, reserving any fat in the frying pan.

2 Peel the onions and cut each into six wedges. Toss with the lamb and roast for about 30-40 minutes, until the lamb is cooked through and the onions are deep golden brown.

3 Tip the lamb and onions back into the frying pan. Mix the harissa with 250ml/8fl oz/1 cup boiling water and add to the roasting pan. Scrape up any residue in the pan and pour the mixture over the lamb and onions. Stir in the prunes and heat until just simmering. Cover and simmer for 5 minutes, then serve.

675g/1½lb lamb fillet or shoulder steaks, cut into chunky pieces

5 small onions

7.5ml/1½ tsp harissa

115g/4oz ready-to-eat pitted prunes, halved

Lamb Steaks with Redcurrant Glaze

This classic, simple dish is absolutely delicious and is an excellent, quick recipe for cooking on the barbecue. The tangy flavour of redcurrants is a traditional accompaniment to lamb. It is good served with new potatoes and fresh garden peas tossed in butter.

SERVES FOUR

1 Reserve the tips of the rosemary and finely chop the remaining leaves. Rub the chopped rosemary, salt and pepper all over the lamb.

2 Preheat the grill (broiler). Heat the redcurrant jelly gently in a small pan with 30ml/2 tbsp water and a little seasoning. Stir in the vinegar.

3 Place the lamb steaks on a foil-lined grill (broiler) rack and brush with a little of the redcurrant glaze. Cook under the grill for about 5 minutes on each side, until deep golden, brushing frequently with more redcurrant glaze.

4 Transfer the lamb to warmed plates. Tip any juices from the foil into the remaining glaze and heat through gently. Pour the glaze over the lamb and serve, garnished with the reserved rosemary sprigs.

4 large fresh rosemary sprigs

4 lamb leg steaks

75ml/5 tbsp redcurrant jelly

30ml/2 tbsp raspberry or red wine vinegar

Paprika Pork

This chunky, goulash-style dish is rich with peppers and paprika. Grilling the peppers before adding them to the meat really brings out their sweet, vibrant flavour. Rice or buttered boiled potatoes go particularly well with the rich pork.

SERVES FOUR

2 red, 1 yellow and 1 green (bell) pepper, seeded

500g/1¼lb lean pork fillet (tenderloin)

45ml/3 tbsp paprika

300g/11oz jar or tub of tomato sauce with herbs or garlic

1 Preheat the grill (broiler). Cut the peppers into thick strips and sprinkle in a single layer on a foil-lined grill rack. Cook under the grill for 20–25 minutes, until the edges of the strips are lightly charred.

2 Meanwhile, cut the pork into chunks. Season with salt and pepper and cook in a non-stick frying pan for about 5 minutes, until beginning to brown.

3 Transfer the meat to a heavy pan and add the paprika, tomato sauce, 300ml/½ pint/1¼ cups water and a little seasoning. Bring to the boil, reduce the heat, cover and simmer gently for 30 minutes.

4 Add the grilled (broiled) peppers and cook for a further 10–15 minutes, until the meat is tender. Taste for seasoning and serve immediately.

Pork Kebabs

The word kebab comes from Arabic and means on a skewer. Use pork fillet (tenderloin) for these kebabs because it is lean and tender, and cooks very quickly. They are good served with rice, or stuffed into warmed pitta bread with some shredded lettuce leaves.

SERVES FOUR

1 Cut the pork into 2.5cm/1in cubes. Cut the spring onions into 2.5cm/1in long sticks.

2 Preheat the grill (broiler) to high. Oil the wire rack and spread out the pork cubes on it. Grill (broil) the pork until the juices drip, then dip the pieces in the barbecue sauce and put back on the grill. Grill for 30 seconds on each side, repeating the dipping process twice more. Set aside and keep warm.

3 Gently grill (broil) the spring onions until soft and slightly brown outside. Do not dip in the barbecue sauce. Thread about four pieces of pork and three spring onion pieces on to each of eight bamboo skewers.

4 Arrange the skewers on a platter. Cut the lemon into wedges and squeeze a little lemon juice over each skewer. Serve immediately, offering the remaining lemon wedges separately.

500g/1¼lb lean pork fillet (tenderloin)

8 large, thick spring onions (scallions), trimmed

120ml/4fl oz/½ cup barbecue sauce

1 lemon

COOK'S TIP
If you are cooking the pork on a barbecue, soak the skewers overnight in water. This prevents them burning. Keep the skewer handles away from the fire and turn them frequently.

Drunken Chicken

In this traditional Chinese dish, cooked chicken is marinated in sherry, fresh root ginger and spring onions for several days. Because of the lengthy preparation time, it is important to use a very fresh bird from a reputable supplier. Fresh herbs can be added as an additional garnish, if you like.

SERVES FOUR TO SIX

1 chicken, about 1.3kg/3lb

1cm/½ in piece of fresh root ginger, thinly sliced

2 spring onions (scallions), trimmed, plus extra to garnish

300ml/½ pint/1¼ cups dry sherry

1 Rinse and dry the chicken inside and out. Place the ginger and spring onions in the body cavity. Put the chicken in a large pan or flameproof casserole and just cover with water. Bring to the boil, skim off any scum and cook for 15 minutes.

2 Turn off the heat, cover the pan or casserole tightly and leave the chicken in the cooking liquid for 3–4 hours, by which time it will be cooked. Drain well, reserving the stock. Pour 300ml/ ½ pint/1¼ cups of the stock into a jug (pitcher).

3 Remove the skin and cut the chicken into neat pieces. Divide each leg into a drumstick and thigh. Make two more portions from the wings and some of the breast. Finally, cut away the remainder of the breast pieces (still on the bone) and divide each piece into two even-size portions.

4 Arrange the chicken portions in a shallow dish. Rub salt into the chicken and cover with clear film (plastic wrap). Leave in a cool place for several hours or overnight in the refrigerator.

5 Later, lift off any fat from the stock, add the sherry and pour over the chicken. Cover again and leave in the refrigerator to marinate for 2–3 days, turning occasionally.

6 When ready to serve, cut the chicken through the bone into chunky pieces and arrange on a large serving platter. Garnish the chicken with spring onion shreds.

VARIATION *To serve as a cocktail snack, take the meat off the bones, cut it into bitesize pieces, then spear each piece on a cocktail stick (toothpick).*

Soy-marinated Chicken

Two simple flavours, soy sauce and orange, combine to make this mouthwatering dish. Serving the chicken on a bed of asparagus turns the dish into a special treat. Wilted spinach or shredded greens work well as an everyday alternative. Boiled egg noodles or steamed white rice make a good accompaniment.

4 skinless, chicken breast fillets

1 large orange

30ml/2 tbsp dark soy sauce

400g/14oz medium asparagus spears

SERVES FOUR

1 Slash each chicken portion diagonally and place them in a single layer in a shallow, ovenproof dish. Halve the orange, squeeze the juice from one half and mix it with the soy sauce. Pour this over the chicken. Cut the remaining orange into wedges and place these on the chicken. Cover and leave to marinate for several hours.

2 Preheat the oven to 180°C/350°F/Gas 4. Turn the chicken over and bake, uncovered, for 20 minutes. Turn the chicken over again and bake for a further 15 minutes, or until cooked through.

3 Meanwhile, cut off any tough ends from the asparagus and place in a frying pan. Pour in enough boiling water just to cover and cook gently for 3–4 minutes, until just tender. Drain and arrange on warmed plates, then top with the chicken and orange wedges. Spoon over the cooking juices and season with black pepper. Serve immediately.

Chicken Escalopes with Lemon and Serrano Ham

Chicken escalopes are flattened chicken breast fillets – they cook quicker than normal breast portions and absorb flavours more readily. In this light summery dish, the chicken absorbs the delicious flavours of the ham and lemon. It can be assembled in advance, so is good for entertaining.

SERVES FOUR

1 Preheat the oven to 180°C/350°F/Gas 4. Beat the butter with plenty of freshly ground black pepper and set aside. Place the chicken portions on a large sheet of clear film (plastic wrap), spacing them well apart. Cover with a second sheet, then beat with a rolling pin until the portions are half their original thickness.

2 Transfer the chicken to a large, shallow ovenproof dish and crumple a slice of ham on top of each. Cut eight thin slices from the lemon and place two on each slice of ham.

3 Dot with the pepper butter and bake for about 30 minutes, until the chicken is cooked. Transfer to serving plates and spoon over any juices from the dish.

40g/1½oz/3 tbsp butter, softened

4 skinless chicken breast fillets

4 slices Serrano ham

1 lemon

Roast Chicken with Herb Cheese, Chilli and Lime Stuffing

Whether you are entertaining guests or cooking a family meal, a tasty chicken is a sure winner every time. This is a modern twist on the classic roast chicken – the stuffing is forced under the chicken skin, which helps to produce a wonderfully flavoured, succulent flesh.

SERVES FIVE TO SIX

1 Preheat the oven to 200°C/400°F/Gas 6. Using first the point of a knife and then your fingers, separate the skin from the meat across the chicken breast and over the tops of the legs. Use the knife to loosen the first piece of skin, then carefully run your fingers underneath, taking care not to tear the skin.

2 Grate the lime and beat the rind into the cream cheese together with the chopped chilli. Pack the cream cheese stuffing under the skin, using a teaspoon, until fairly evenly distributed. Push the skin back into place, then smooth your hands over it to spread the stuffing in an even layer.

3 Put the chicken in a roasting pan and squeeze the juice from the lime over the top. Roast for 1½ hours, or until the juices run clear when the thickest part of the thigh is pierced with a skewer. If necessary, cover the chicken with foil towards the end of cooking if the top starts to become too browned.

4 Carve the chicken and arrange on a warmed serving platter. Spoon the pan juices over it and serve immediately.

1.8kg/4lb chicken

1 lime

115g/4oz/½ cup cream cheese with herbs and garlic

1 mild fresh red chilli, seeded and finely chopped

Turkey Patties

So much better than store-bought burgers, these light patties are delicious served hamburger-style in split and toasted buns with relish, salad leaves and chunky fries. They can also be made using minced chicken, lamb, pork or beef. If you are making them for children, shape the mixture into 12 equal-sized rounds and serve in mini-rolls or in rounds stamped out from sliced bread.

SERVES SIX

675g/1½lb minced (ground) turkey

1 small red onion, finely chopped

small handful of fresh thyme leaves

30ml/2 tbsp lime-flavoured olive oil

1 Mix together the turkey, onion, thyme, 15ml/1 tbsp of the oil and seasoning. Cover and chill for up to 4 hours to let the flavours infuse (steep), then divide the mixture into six equal portions and shape into round patties.

2 Preheat a griddle pan. Brush the patties with half of the remaining lime-flavoured olive oil, then place them on the pan and cook for 10–12 minutes. Turn the patties over, brush with more oil, and cook for 10–12 minutes on the second side, or until cooked right through. Serve the patties immediately.

VARIATION *As well as using other minced (ground) meat, you could try chopped oregano or parsley in place of the thyme, and lemon-flavoured oil instead of lime.*

Guinea Fowl with Whisky Sauce

Served with creamy, sweet mashed potato and lightly boiled whole baby leeks, guinea fowl is magnificent with a rich, creamy whisky sauce. If you don't like the flavour of whisky, then substitute brandy, Madeira or Marsala. Or, to make a non-alcoholic version, use freshly squeezed orange juice instead. Garnish with fresh thyme sprigs or other fresh herbs.

SERVES FOUR

2 guinea fowl, each weighing about 1kg/2¼lb

90ml/6 tbsp whisky

150ml/¼ pint/⅔ cup well-flavoured chicken stock

150ml/¼ pint/⅔ cup double (heavy) cream

1 Preheat the oven to 200°C/400°F/Gas 6. Brown the guinea fowl on all sides in a roasting pan on the hob (stovetop), then turn it breast uppermost and transfer the pan to the oven. Roast for about 1 hour, until the guinea fowl are golden and cooked through. Transfer the guinea fowl to a warmed serving dish, cover with foil and keep warm.

2 Pour off the excess fat from the pan, then heat the juices on the hob and stir in the whisky. Bring to the boil and cook until reduced. Add the stock and cream and simmer again until reduced slightly. Strain and season to taste.

3 Carve the guinea fowl and serve on individual plates, arranged around the chosen vegetable accompaniments. Sprinkle with plenty of freshly ground black pepper. Spoon a little of the sauce over each portion and serve the rest separately.

Pheasant Cooked in Port with Mushrooms

This warming dish is delicious served with mashed root vegetables and shredded cabbage or leeks. Marinating the pheasant in port helps to moisten and tenderize the meat, which can often be slightly dry. If you prefer, marinate the pheasant in a full-bodied red wine and use button (white) mushrooms.

SERVES FOUR

2 pheasants, cut into portions

300ml/½ pint/1¼ cups port

50g/2oz/¼ cup butter

300g/11oz chestnut mushrooms, halved if large

1 Place the pheasant in a bowl and pour over the port. Cover and marinate for 3–4 hours or overnight, turning the portions occasionally.

2 Drain the meat thoroughly, reserving the marinade. Pat the portions dry on kitchen paper and season lightly with salt and pepper. Melt three-quarters of the butter in a frying pan and cook the pheasant portions on all sides for about 5 minutes, until deep golden. Drain well, transfer to a plate, then cook the mushrooms in the fat remaining in the pan for 3 minutes.

3 Return the pheasant to the pan and pour in the reserved marinade with 200ml/7fl oz/scant 1 cup water. Bring to the boil, reduce the heat and cover, then simmer gently for about 45 minutes, until the pheasant is tender.

4 Using a slotted spoon, carefully remove the pheasant portions and mushrooms from the frying pan and keep warm. Bring the cooking juices to the boil and boil vigorously for 3–5 minutes, until they are reduced and slightly thickened. Strain the juices through a fine sieve and return them to the pan. Whisk in the remaining butter over a gentle heat until it has melted, season to taste, then pour the juices over the pheasant and mushrooms and serve.

Duck with Plum Sauce

Sharp plums cut the rich flavour of duck wonderfully well in this updated version of an old English dish. Duck is often considered to be a fatty meat but modern breeding methods have made leaner ducks widely available. For an easy dinner party main course, serve the duck with creamy mashed potatoes and celeriac and steamed broccoli.

SERVES FOUR

4 duck quarters

1 large red onion, finely chopped

500g/1¼lb ripe plums, stoned (pitted) and quartered

30ml/2 tbsp redcurrant jelly

1 Prick the duck skin all over with a fork to release the fat during cooking and help give a crisp result, then place the portions in a heavy frying pan, skin side down.

2 Cook the duck pieces for 10 minutes on each side, or until golden brown and cooked right through. Remove the duck from the frying pan using a slotted spoon and keep warm.

3 Pour away all but 30ml/2 tbsp of the duck fat, then stir-fry the onion for 5 minutes, or until golden. Add the plums and cook for 5 minutes, stirring frequently. Add the jelly and mix well.

4 Replace the duck portions and cook for a further 5 minutes, or until thoroughly reheated. Season to taste before serving.

COOK'S TIP *It is important that the plums used in this dish are very ripe, otherwise the mixture will be too dry and the sauce will be extremely sharp.*

Vegetarian Dishes

FRESH-TASTING VEGETABLES, MILD EGGS,

RICH AND CREAMY CHEESES AND AROMATIC HERBS

AND SPICES ARE GREAT PARTNERS AND CAN BE COMBINED

TO MAKE A DELICIOUS ARRAY OF VEGETARIAN MEALS.

ENJOY WONDERFUL DISHES SUCH AS BAKED

STUFFED VEGETABLES, RICHLY FLAVOURED TARTS

AND LIGHT-AS-AIR SOUFFLÉS.

Aubergines with Cheese Sauce

This wonderfully simple dish of aubergines in cheese sauce is delicious hot and the perfect dish to assemble ahead of time ready for baking at the last minute. Kashkaval cheese is particularly good in this recipe – it is a hard yellow cheese made from sheep's milk and is originally from the Balkans. Serve with lots of crusty bread to mop up the delicious aubergine-flavoured cheese sauce.

SERVES FOUR TO SIX

1 Layer the aubergine slices in a bowl or colander, sprinkling each layer with salt, and leave to drain for at least 30 minutes. Rinse well, then pat dry with kitchen paper.

2 Heat the oil in a frying pan, then cook the aubergine slices until golden brown on both sides. Remove from the pan and set aside.

3 Preheat the oven to 180°C/350°F/Gas 4. Mix most of the grated cheese into the savoury white or béchamel sauce, reserving a little to sprinkle on top of the finished dish.

4 Arrange a layer of the aubergines in an ovenproof dish, then pour over some sauce. Repeat, ending with sauce. Sprinkle with the reserved cheese. Bake for 35–40 minutes until golden.

2 large aubergines (eggplant), cut into 5mm/¼ in thick slices

about 60ml/4 tbsp olive oil

400g/14oz/3½ cups grated cheese, such as kashkaval, Gruyère, or a mixture of Parmesan and Cheddar

600ml/1 pint/2½ cups savoury white sauce or béchamel sauce

Mushroom Stroganoff

This creamy mixed mushroom sauce is ideal for a dinner party. Serve it with toasted buckwheat, brown rice or a mixture of wild rices and garnish with snipped chives. For best results, choose a variety of different mushrooms – wild mushrooms such as chanterelles, ceps and morels add a delicious flavour and texture to the stroganoff, as well as adding colour and producing a decorative appearance.

SERVES FOUR

25g/1oz/2 tbsp butter

900g/2lb mixed mushrooms, cut into bitesize pieces, including ⅔ button (white) mushrooms and ⅓ assorted wild or unusual mushrooms

350ml/12fl oz/ 1½ cups white wine sauce

250ml/8fl oz/1 cup sour cream

1 Melt the butter in a pan and quickly cook the mushrooms, in batches, over a high heat, until brown. Transfer the mushrooms to a bowl after cooking each batch.

2 Add the sauce to the juices remaining in the pan and bring to the boil, stirring. Reduce the heat and replace the mushrooms with any juices from the bowl. Stir well and heat for a few seconds, then remove from the heat.

3 Stir the sour cream into the cooked mushroom mixture and season to taste with salt and lots of freshly ground black pepper. Heat through gently for a few seconds, if necessary, then transfer to warm plates and serve immediately.

Red Onion and Goat's Cheese Pastries

These attractive little tartlets couldn't be easier to make. Garnish them with fresh thyme sprigs and serve with a selection of salad leaves and a tomato and basil salad for a light lunch or quick supper. A wide variety of different types of goat's cheeses are available – the creamy log-shaped types without a rind are most suitable for these pastries. Ordinary onions can be used instead of red, if you prefer.

SERVES FOUR

1 Heat the oil in a large, heavy frying pan, add the onions and cook over a gentle heat for 10 minutes, or until softened, stirring occasionally to prevent them from browning. Add seasoning to taste and cook for a further 2 minutes. Remove the pan from the heat and leave to cool.

2 Preheat the oven to 220°C/425°F/Gas 7. Unroll the puff pastry and using a 15cm/6in plate as a guide, cut out four rounds. Place the pastry rounds on a dampened baking sheet and, using the point of a sharp knife, score a border, 2cm/¾in inside the edge of each pastry round.

3 Divide the onions among the pastry rounds and top with the goat's cheese. Bake for 25–30 minutes until golden brown.

15ml/1 tbsp olive oil

450g/1lb red onions, sliced

425g/15oz packet ready-rolled puff pastry

115g/4oz/1 cup goat's cheese, cubed

EXTRAS *To make richer-flavoured pastries ring the changes by spreading the pastry base with red or green pesto or tapenade before you top with the goat's cheese and cooked onions.*

Baked Leek and Potato Gratin

Potatoes baked in a creamy cheese sauce make the ultimate comfort dish, whether served as an accompaniment to pork or fish dishes or, as here, with plenty of leeks and melted cheese as a main course. When preparing leeks, separate the leaves and rinse them thoroughly under cold running water, as soil and grit often get caught between the layers.

SERVES FOUR TO SIX

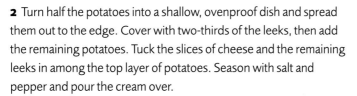

1 Preheat the oven to 180°C/350°F/Gas 4. Cook the potatoes in plenty of lightly salted, boiling water for 3 minutes, until slightly softened, then drain. Cut the leeks into 1cm/½in lengths and blanch them in boiling water for 1 minute, until softened, then drain.

2 Turn half the potatoes into a shallow, ovenproof dish and spread them out to the edge. Cover with two-thirds of the leeks, then add the remaining potatoes. Tuck the slices of cheese and the remaining leeks in among the top layer of potatoes. Season with salt and pepper and pour the cream over.

3 Bake for 1 hour, until tender and golden. Cover with foil if the top starts to overbrown before the potatoes are tender.

900g/2lb medium potatoes, thinly sliced

2 large leeks, trimmed

200g/7oz ripe Brie or Camembert cheese, sliced

450ml/¾ pint/ scant 2 cups single (light) cream

Mushroom Polenta

This simple recipe uses freshly made polenta, but for an even easier version you can substitute ready-made polenta and slice it straight into the dish, ready for baking. The cheesy mushroom topping is also delicious on toasted herb or sun-dried tomato bread as a light lunch or supper. Any combination of mushrooms will work – try a mixture of button (white) and wild mushrooms as an alternative.

SERVES FOUR

1 Line a 28 x 18cm/11 x 7in shallow baking tin (pan) with baking parchment. Bring 1 litre/1¾ pints/4 cups water with 5ml/1 tsp salt to the boil in a large pan. Add the polenta in a steady stream, stirring constantly. Bring back to the boil, stirring, and cook for 5 minutes, until thick and smooth. Turn the polenta into the prepared tin and spread it out into an even layer. Leave to cool.

2 Preheat the oven to 200°C/400°F/Gas 6. Melt the butter in a frying pan and cook the mushrooms for 3–5 minutes, until golden. Season with salt and lots of freshly ground black pepper.

3 Turn out the polenta on to a chopping board. Peel away the parchment and cut the polenta into large squares. Pile the squares into a shallow, ovenproof dish. Sprinkle with half the cheese, then pile the mushrooms on top and pour over their buttery juices. Sprinkle with the remaining cheese and bake for about 20 minutes, until the cheese is melting and pale golden.

250g/9oz/1½ cups quick-cook polenta

50g/2oz/ ¼ cup butter

400g/14oz chestnut mushrooms, sliced

175g/6oz/1½ cups grated Gruyère cheese

Tomato and Tapenade Tarts

These delicious individual tarts look and taste fantastic, despite the fact that they demand very little time or effort. The mascarpone cheese topping melts as it cooks to make a smooth, creamy sauce. Cherry tomatoes have a delicious sweet flavour with a low acidity, but plum tomatoes or vine-ripened tomatoes are also suitable for these tarts and will give delicious results. Red pesto can be used instead of the tapenade if you prefer a subtler flavour.

SERVES FOUR

1 Preheat the oven to 220°C/425°F/Gas 7. Lightly grease a large baking sheet and sprinkle it with water. Roll out the pastry on a lightly floured surface and cut out four 16cm/6½in rounds, using a bowl or small plate as a guide.

2 Transfer the pastry rounds to the prepared baking sheet. Using the tip of a sharp knife, mark a shallow cut 1cm/½in in from the edge of each round to form a rim.

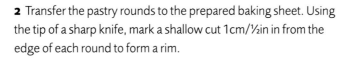

3 Reserve half the tapenade and spread the rest over the pastry rounds, keeping the paste inside the marked rim. Cut half the tomatoes in half. Pile all the tomatoes, whole and halved, on the pastry, again keeping them inside the rim. Season lightly.

4 Bake for 20 minutes, until the pastry is well risen and golden. Dot with the remaining tapenade. Spoon a little mascarpone on the centre of the tomatoes and season with black pepper. Bake for a further 10 minutes, until the mascarpone has melted to make a sauce. Serve the tarts warm.

500g/1¼lb puff pastry, thawed if frozen

60ml/4 tbsp black or green olive tapenade

500g/1¼lb cherry tomatoes

90g/3½oz/scant ½ cup mascarpone cheese

Stuffed Baby Squash

It is worth making the most of baby squash while they are in season. Use any varieties you can find and do not worry too much about choosing vegetables of uniform size, as an assortment of different types and sizes looks attractive. The baked vegetables can easily be shared out at the table. Serve with warm sun-dried tomato bread and a ready-made spicy tomato sauce for a hearty autumn supper.

SERVES FOUR

1 Preheat the oven to 190°C/375°F/Gas 5. Pierce the squash in several places with the tip of a knife. Bake for 30 minutes, until the squash are tender. Leave until cool enough to handle.

2 Meanwhile, cook the rice in salted, boiling water for 12 minutes, until tender, then drain. Slice a lid off the top of each squash and scoop out and discard the seeds. Scoop out and chop the flesh.

3 Heat the oil in a frying pan and cook the chopped squash for 5 minutes. Reserve 60ml/4 tbsp of the cheese, add the remainder to the pan with the rice and a little salt. Mix well.

4 Pile the mixture into the squash shells and place in an ovenproof dish. Sprinkle with the remaining cheese and bake for 20 minutes.

4 small squash, each about 350g/12oz

200g/7oz/1 cup mixed wild and basmati rice

60ml/4 tbsp chilli and garlic oil

150g/5oz/1¼ cups grated Gruyère cheese

Roasted Peppers with Halloumi and Pine Nuts

Halloumi cheese is creamy-tasting and has a firm texture and salty flavour that contrast well with the succulent sweet peppers. This is a good dish to assemble in advance. Halloumi is usually served cooked and lends itself well to barbecuing, frying or grilling (broiling). When heated the exterior hardens while the interior softens and is similar to mozzarella cheese.

SERVES FOUR

1 Preheat the oven to 220°C/425°F/Gas 7. Halve the red peppers, leaving the stalks intact, and discard the seeds. Seed and coarsely chop the orange or yellow peppers. Place the red pepper halves on a baking sheet and fill with the chopped peppers. Drizzle with half the garlic or herb olive oil and bake for 25 minutes, until the edges of the peppers are beginning to char.

2 Dice the cheese and tuck in among the chopped peppers. Sprinkle with the pine nuts and drizzle with the remaining oil. Bake for a further 15 minutes, until well browned. Serve warm.

4 red and 2 orange or yellow (bell) peppers

60ml/4 tbsp garlic or herb olive oil

250g/9oz halloumi cheese

50g/2oz/½ cup pine nuts

Spicy Chickpea Samosas

A blend of crushed chickpeas and coriander sauce makes an interesting alternative to the more familiar meat or vegetable fillings in these little pastries. The samosas look pretty garnished with fresh coriander leaves and finely sliced onion and are delicious served with a simple dip made from Greek (US strained plain) yogurt and chopped fresh mint leaves.

MAKES EIGHTEEN

1 Preheat the oven to 220°C/425°F/Gas 7. Process half the chickpeas to a paste in a food processor. Tip the paste into a bowl and add the whole chickpeas, the hara masala or coriander sauce, and a little salt. Mix until well combined.

2 Lay a sheet of filo pastry on a work surface and cut into three strips. Brush the strips with a little of the oil. Place a dessertspoon of the filling at one end of a strip. Turn one corner diagonally over the filling to meet the long edge. Continue folding the filling and the pastry along the length of the strip, keeping the triangular shape. Transfer to a baking sheet and repeat with the remaining filling and pastry.

3 Brush the pastries with any remaining oil and bake for 15 minutes, until the pastry is golden. Cool slightly before serving.

2 x 400g/14oz cans chickpeas, drained and rinsed

120ml/4fl oz/½ cup hara masala or coriander (cilantro) sauce

275g/10oz filo pastry

60ml/4 tbsp chilli and garlic oil

Tofu and Pepper Kebabs

A simple coating of ground, dry-roasted peanuts pressed on to cubed tofu provides plenty of additional flavour along with the peppers. Use metal or bamboo skewers for the kebabs – if you use bamboo, then soak them in cold water for 30 minutes before using to prevent them from scorching during cooking. The kebabs can also be cooked on a barbecue, if you prefer.

SERVES FOUR

1 Pat the tofu dry on kitchen paper and then cut it into small cubes. Grind the peanuts in a blender or food processor and transfer to a plate. Turn the tofu cubes in the ground nuts to coat.

2 Preheat the grill (broiler) to moderate. Halve and seed the peppers, and cut them into large chunks. Thread the chunks of pepper on to four large skewers with the tofu cubes and place on a foil-lined grill rack.

3 Grill (broil) the kebabs, turning frequently, for 10–12 minutes, or until the peppers and peanuts are beginning to brown. Transfer the kebabs to plates and serve with the dipping sauce.

250g/9oz firm tofu

50g/2oz/½ cup dry-roasted peanuts

2 red and 2 green (bell) peppers

60ml/4 tbsp sweet chilli dipping sauce

Mixed Bean and Tomato Chilli

Here, mixed beans, fiery red chilli and plenty of freshly chopped coriander are simmered in a tomato sauce to make a delicious vegetarian chilli. Always a popular dish, chilli can be served with a variety of accompaniments – choose from baked potatoes, baked rice, crusty bread or tortillas. Garnish with slices of tomato, chopped celery or sweet (bell) pepper and top with natural (plain) yogurt.

SERVES FOUR

1 Pour the tomato sauce and mixed beans into a pan. Seed and thinly slice the chilli, then add it to the pan. Reserve a little of the coriander, chop the remainder and add it to the pan.

2 Bring the mixture to the boil, reduce the heat, cover and simmer gently for 10 minutes. Stir the mixture occasionally and add a dash of water if the sauce starts to dry out.

3 Ladle the chilli into warmed individual serving bowls and top with a spoonful of yogurt to serve.

400g/14oz jar tomato and herb sauce

2 x 400g/14oz cans mixed beans, drained and rinsed

1 fresh red chilli

large handful of fresh coriander (cilantro)

Cheese and Tomato Soufflés

Using a ready-made cheese sauce takes the effort out of soufflé making. The key to success when making soufflés is to whisk the egg whites thoroughly to incorporate as much air as possible. During the cooking time don't open the oven door – the cold draught could cause the delicate mixture to collapse.

SERVES SIX

1 Preheat the oven to 200°C/400°F/Gas 6. Turn the cheese sauce into a bowl. Thinly slice the sun-dried tomatoes and add to the bowl with 90g/3½oz/generous 1 cup of the Parmesan, the egg yolks and seasoning. Stir until well combined.

2 Brush the base and sides of six 200ml/7fl oz/scant 1 cup ramekins with the oil and then coat the insides of the dishes with half the remaining cheese, tilting them until evenly covered.

3 Whisk the egg whites in a clean bowl until stiff. Use a large metal spoon to stir one-quarter of the egg whites into the sauce, then fold in the remainder. Spoon the mixture into the prepared dishes and sprinkle with the remaining Parmesan cheese. Place on a baking sheet and bake for 15–18 minutes, until well risen and golden. Serve the soufflés as soon as you remove them from the oven.

350g/12oz tub fresh cheese sauce

50g/2oz sun-dried tomatoes in olive oil, drained, plus 10ml/ 2 tsp of the oil

130g/4½oz/1⅓ cups grated Parmesan cheese

4 large (US extra large) eggs, separated

Potato and Onion Tortilla

This deep-set omelette with sliced potatoes and onions is the best-known Spanish tortilla and makes a deliciously simple meal when served with a leafy salad and crusty bread. Tortilla are often made with a variety of ingredients – chopped red or yellow (bell) peppers, cooked peas, corn, or grated Cheddar or Gruyère cheese can all be added to the mixture in step 2, if you like.

SERVES FOUR TO SIX

800g/1¾ lb medium potatoes

100ml/3½fl oz/ scant ½ cup extra virgin olive oil

2 onions, thinly sliced

6 eggs

1 Thinly slice the potatoes. Heat 75ml/5 tbsp of the oil in a frying pan and cook the potatoes, turning frequently, for 10 minutes. Add the onions and seasoning, and continue to cook gently for a further 10 minutes, until the vegetables are tender.

2 Meanwhile, beat the eggs in a large bowl with a little seasoning. Tip the potatoes and onions into the eggs and mix gently. Leave to stand for 10 minutes.

3 Wipe out the pan with kitchen paper and heat the remaining oil in it. Pour the egg mixture into the pan and spread it out in an even layer. Cover and cook over a very gentle heat for 20 minutes, until the eggs are just set. Serve cut into wedges.

Spiced Lentils

The combination of lentils, tomatoes and cheese is widely used in Mediterranean cooking. The tang of feta cheese complements the slightly earthy flavour of the attractive dark lentils. True Puy lentils come from the region of France, Le Puy, which has a unique climate and volcanic soil in which they thrive.

SERVES FOUR

250g/9oz/1½ cups Puy lentils

200g/7oz feta cheese

75ml/5 tbsp sun-dried tomato purée (paste)

small handful of fresh chervil or flat leaf parsley, chopped, plus extra to garnish

1 Place the lentils in a heavy pan with 600ml/1 pint/2½ cups water. Bring to the boil, reduce the heat and cover the pan. Simmer gently for about 20 minutes, until the lentils are just tender and most of the water has been absorbed.

2 Crumble half the feta cheese into the pan. Add the sun-dried tomato purée, chopped chervil or flat leaf parsley and a little salt and freshly ground black pepper. Heat through for 1 minute.

3 Transfer the lentil mixture and juices to warmed plates or bowls. Crumble the remaining feta cheese on top and sprinkle with the fresh herbs to garnish. Serve the lentils immediately.

Pasta and Rice Dishes

PASTA AND RICE ARE THE PERFECT STAPLES UPON WHICH
TO BASE SIMPLE, TASTY MEALS. YOU NEED ONLY A FEW
INGREDIENTS TO RUSTLE UP DELICIOUS DISHES, FROM A
SIMPLE MIDWEEK SUPPER TO MORE ELEGANT DISHES FOR
ENTERTAINING. WHETHER YOU CHOOSE A SUBSTANTIAL
BOWL OF PASTA OR A FRAGRANT SEAFOOD RISOTTO –
THE RECIPES IN THIS CHAPTER ARE SURE TO DELIGHT.

Spaghettini with Roasted Garlic

If you have never tried roasting garlic, then this is the recipe that will convert you to its delicious mellowed sweetness. Spaghettini is very fine spaghetti, but any long thin pasta can be used in this dish – try spaghetti, linguine, tagliatelle or capellini. This simple pasta dish is very good served with a mixed leaf salad dressed with lemon juice and extra virgin olive oil.

SERVES FOUR

1 Preheat the oven to 180°C/350°F/Gas 4. Place the garlic in an oiled roasting pan and roast it for 30 minutes.

2 Leave the garlic to cool, then lay it on its side and slice off the top one-third with a sharp knife.

3 Hold the garlic over a bowl and dig out the flesh from each clove with the point of the knife. When all the flesh has been added to the bowl, pour in the oil and add plenty of black pepper. Mix well.

4 Cook the pasta in a pan of salted boiling water according to the instructions on the packet. Drain the pasta and return it to the clean pan. Pour in the oil and garlic mixture and toss the pasta vigorously over a medium heat until all the strands are thoroughly coated. Serve immediately, with shavings of Parmesan.

1 whole head of garlic

120ml/4fl oz/½ cup extra virgin olive oil

400g/14oz fresh or dried spaghettini

coarsely shaved Parmesan cheese

EXTRAS *For a fiery finish, sprinkle crushed, dried red chillies over the pasta when tossing it with the oil and garlic.*

Spaghetti with Lemon

This is the dish to make when you get home and find there's nothing to eat. If you keep spaghetti and olive oil in the storecupboard (pantry), and garlic and lemons in the vegetable rack, you can prepare this delicious meal in minutes. You can also add some freshly grated Parmesan cheese if you have some.

SERVES FOUR

1 Cook the pasta in a pan of salted boiling water according to the instructions on the packet, then drain well and return to the pan.

2 Pour the olive oil and lemon juice over the cooked pasta, sprinkle in the slivers of garlic and add seasoning to taste. Toss the pasta over a medium to high heat for 1–2 minutes. Serve immediately in four warmed bowls.

350g/12oz dried spaghetti

90ml/6 tbsp extra virgin olive oil

juice of 1 large lemon

2 garlic cloves, cut into very thin slivers

COOK'S TIP *Spaghetti is the best type of pasta for this recipe, because the olive oil and lemon juice cling to its long thin strands. If you are out of spaghetti, use another dried long pasta shape instead, such as spaghettini, linguine or tagliatelle.*

Linguine with Rocket

This fashionable first course is very quick and easy to make at home. Rocket has an excellent peppery flavour which combines beautifully with the rich, creamy tang of fresh Parmesan cheese. Fresh Parmesan keeps well in the refrigerator for up to a month – the dried variety is a very poor substitute and bears little resemblance to the real thing.

SERVES FOUR

1 Cook the pasta in a large pan of lightly salted boiling water according to the instructions on the packet, then drain thoroughly.

2 Heat about 60ml/4 tbsp of the olive oil in the pasta pan, then add the drained pasta, followed by the rocket. Toss over a medium to high heat for 1–2 minutes, or until the rocket is just wilted, then remove the pan from the heat.

3 Tip the pasta and rocket into a large, warmed bowl. Add half the freshly grated Parmesan and the remaining olive oil. Add a little salt and black pepper to taste.

4 Toss the mixture quickly to mix. Serve immediately, sprinkled with the remaining Parmesan.

350g/12oz fresh or dried linguine

120ml/4fl oz/½ cup extra virgin olive oil

1 large bunch rocket (arugula), about 150g/5oz, stalks removed, shredded or torn

75g/3oz/1 cup freshly grated Parmesan cheese

Tagliatelle with Vegetable Ribbons

Narrow strips of courgette and carrot mingle well with tagliatelle to resemble coloured pasta. Serve as a side dish, or sprinkle with freshly grated Parmesan cheese for a light appetizer or vegetarian main course. Garlic flavoured olive oil is used in this dish – flavoured oils such as rosemary, chilli or basil are widely available and are a quick way of adding flavour to pasta.

SERVES FOUR

2 large courgettes (zucchini)

2 large carrots

250g/9oz fresh egg tagliatelle

60ml/4 tbsp garlic flavoured olive oil

1 With a vegetable peeler, cut the courgettes and carrots into long thin ribbons. Bring a large pan of salted water to the boil, then add the courgette and carrot ribbons. Bring the water back to the boil and boil for 30 seconds, then drain and set aside.

2 Cook the tagliatelle according to the instructions on the packet. Drain the pasta and return it to the pan. Add the vegetable ribbons, garlic flavoured oil and seasoning and toss over a medium to high heat until the pasta and vegetables are glistening with oil. Serve the pasta immediately.

Spaghetti with Raw Tomato and Ricotta Sauce

This wonderfully simple uncooked sauce goes well with many different kinds of freshly cooked pasta, both long strands such as spaghetti, tagliatelle or linguini, and short shapes such as macaroni, rigatoni or penne. It is always at its best in summer when made with rich, sweet plum tomatoes that have ripened on the vine in the sun and have their fullest flavour.

SERVES FOUR

500g/1¼ lb ripe Italian plum tomatoes

75ml/5 tbsp garlic-flavoured olive oil

350g/12oz dried spaghetti or pasta of your choice

115g/4oz ricotta salata cheese, diced

1 Coarsely chop the plum tomatoes, removing the cores and as many of the seeds as you can.

2 Put the tomatoes and oil in a bowl, adding salt and pepper to taste, and stir well. Cover and leave at room temperature for 1–2 hours to let the flavours mingle.

3 Cook the spaghetti or your chosen pasta according to the packet instructions, then drain well.

4 Taste the sauce to check the seasoning before tossing it with the hot pasta. Sprinkle with the cheese and serve immediately.

Farfalle with Tuna

Bought tomato sauce and canned tuna are endlessly versatile for making weekday suppers. A variety of herbs can be added to simple pasta dishes like this one – choose from basil, marjoram or oregano – and use fresh herbs, as the short cooking time does not allow the flavour of dried herbs to develop fully. Add a garnish of fresh oregano to this dish if you happen to have some.

SERVES FOUR

1 Cook the pasta in a large pan of lightly salted boiling water according to the instructions on the packet. Meanwhile, heat the tomato sauce in a separate pan and add the olives.

2 Drain the canned tuna and flake it with a fork. Add the tuna to the sauce with about 60ml/4 tbsp of the hot water used for cooking the pasta. Taste and adjust the seasoning.

3 Drain the pasta thoroughly and tip it into a large, warmed serving bowl. Pour the tuna sauce over the top and toss lightly to mix. Serve immediately.

400g/14oz/3½ cups dried farfalle

600ml/1 pint/2½ cups tomato sauce

175g/6oz can tuna in olive oil

8–10 pitted black olives, cut into rings

Fettucine all'Alfredo

This simple recipe was invented by a Roman restaurateur called Alfredo, who became famous for serving it with a gold fork and spoon. Today's busy cooks will find cartons of long-life cream invaluable for this type of recipe. If you can't get fettucine, any long ribbon-like pasta can be used in this dish – try tagliatelle or slightly wider pappardelle instead.

SERVES FOUR

1 Melt the butter in a large pan. Add the cream and bring it to the boil. Simmer for 5 minutes, stirring constantly, then add the Parmesan cheese, with salt and freshly ground black pepper to taste, and turn off the heat under the pan.

2 Bring a large pan of salted water to the boil. Drop in the pasta all at once and quickly bring the water back to the boil, stirring occasionally. Cook the pasta for 2–3 minutes, or according to the instructions on the packet. Drain well.

3 Turn on the heat under the pan of cream to low, add the cooked pasta all at once and toss until it is thoroughly coated in the sauce. Taste the sauce for seasoning. Serve immediately, with extra grated Parmesan handed around separately.

50g/2oz/¼ cup butter

200ml/7fl oz/ scant 1 cup double (heavy) cream

50g/2oz/⅔ cup freshly grated Parmesan cheese, plus extra to serve

350g/12oz fresh fettucine

Pansotti with Walnut Sauce

Walnuts and cream make a rich and luscious sauce for stuffed pasta, particularly the types filled with cheese and herbs. Serve this indulgent dish with warm walnut bread and a light, fruity white wine.

SERVES FOUR

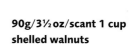

1 Put the walnuts and garlic oil in a food processor and process to a paste, adding up to 120ml/4fl oz/½ cup warm water through the feeder tube to slacken the consistency. Spoon the mixture into a large bowl and add the cream. Beat well to mix, then season to taste with salt and black pepper.

2 Cook the pansotti or stuffed pasta in a large pan of salted boiling water for 4–5 minutes, or according to the instructions on the packet. Meanwhile, put the walnut sauce in a large warmed bowl and add a ladleful of the pasta cooking water to thin it.

3 Drain the pasta and tip it into the bowl of walnut sauce. Toss well, then serve immediately.

90g/3½oz/scant 1 cup shelled walnuts

60ml/4 tbsp garlic-flavoured olive oil

120ml/4fl oz/½ cup double (heavy) cream

350g/12oz cheese and herb-filled pansotti or other stuffed pasta

Rosemary Risotto with Borlotti Beans

Select a high-quality risotto in a subtle flavour as the base for this recipe. The savoury beans, heady rosemary and creamy mascarpone will transform a simple product into a feast. For an even more authentic risotto flavour, substitute half the water with dry white wine. Serve with a simple salad of rocket (arugula) and Parmesan shavings dressed with balsamic vinegar and plenty of freshly ground black pepper.

SERVES THREE TO FOUR

400g/14oz can borlotti beans

275g/10oz packet vegetable or chicken risotto

60ml/4 tbsp mascarpone cheese

5ml/1 tsp finely chopped fresh rosemary

1 Drain the beans, rinse under cold water and drain again. Process about two-thirds of the beans to a fairly coarse purée in a food processor or blender. Set the remaining beans aside.

2 Make up the risotto according to the packet instructions, using the suggested quantity of water.

3 Immediately the rice is cooked, stir in the bean purée. Add the reserved beans, with the mascarpone and rosemary, then season to taste. Stir thoroughly, then cover and leave to stand for about 5 minutes so that the risotto absorbs the flavours fully.

VARIATION

Fresh thyme or marjoram could be used for this risotto instead of rosemary, if you like. One of the great virtues of risotto is that it lends itself well to many variations. Experiment with plain or saffron risotto and add different herbs to make your own speciality dish.

Pancetta and Broad Bean Risotto

This moist risotto makes a satisfying, balanced meal, especially when served with cooked fresh seasonal vegetables or a mixed green salad. Add some chopped fresh herbs and Parmesan shavings as a garnish, if you like. Pancetta is dry cured pork and is the Italian equivalent of streaky (fatty) bacon – either can be used in this recipe.

SERVES FOUR

175g/6oz smoked pancetta, diced

350g/12oz/1¾ cups risotto rice

1.5 litres/2½ pints/ 6 ¼ cups simmering herb stock

225g/8oz/2 cups frozen baby broad (fava) beans

1 Place the pancetta in a non-stick or heavy pan and cook gently, stirring occasionally, for about 5 minutes, until the fat runs.

2 Add the risotto rice to the pan and cook for 1 minute, stirring constantly. Add a ladleful of the simmering stock and cook, stirring constantly, until the liquid has been absorbed.

3 Continue adding the simmering stock, a ladleful at a time, until the rice is tender, and almost all the liquid has been absorbed. This will take 30–35 minutes.

4 Meanwhile, cook the broad beans in a pan of lightly salted, boiling water for about 3 minutes until tender. Drain well and stir into the risotto. Season to taste. Spoon into a bowl and serve.

COOK'S TIP *If the broad beans are large, or if you prefer skinned beans, remove the outer skin after cooking them.*

Mussel Risotto

The addition of freshly cooked mussels, aromatic coriander and a little cream to a packet of instant risotto can turn a simple meal into a decadent treat. Serve with a side salad for a splendid supper. Other types of cooked shellfish, such as clams or prawns (shrimp), can be used instead of mussels.

SERVES THREE TO FOUR

1 Scrub the mussels, discarding any that do not close when sharply tapped. Place in a large pan. Add 120ml/4fl oz/½ cup water and seasoning, then bring to the boil. Cover the pan and cook the mussels, shaking the pan occasionally, for 4–5 minutes, until they have opened. Drain, reserving the liquid and discarding any that have not opened. Shell most of the mussels, reserving a few in their shells for garnish. Strain the mussel liquid.

2 Make up the packet risotto according to the instructions, using the cooking liquid from the mussels and making it up to the required volume with water.

3 When the risotto is about three-quarters cooked, add the mussels to the pan. Add the coriander and re-cover the pan without stirring in these ingredients.

4 Remove the risotto from the heat, stir in the cream, cover and leave to rest for a few minutes. Spoon into a warmed serving dish, garnish with the reserved mussels in their shells, and serve.

900g/2lb fresh mussels

275g/10oz packet risotto

30ml/2 tbsp chopped fresh coriander (cilantro)

30ml/2 tbsp double (heavy) cream

COOK'S TIP *For a super-quick mussel risotto, use cooked mussels in their shells – the type sold vacuum packed ready to reheat. Just reheat them according to the packet instructions and add to the made risotto with the coriander and cream.*

Crab Risotto

This simple risotto has a subtle flavour that makes the most of delicate crab. It makes a tempting main course or appetizer. It is important to use a good quality risotto rice, which will give a deliciously creamy result, but the cooked grains are still firm to the bite.

SERVES THREE TO FOUR

2 large cooked crabs

275g/10oz/1½ cups risotto rice

1.2 litres/2 pints/ 5 cups simmering fish stock

30ml/2 tbsp mixed finely chopped fresh herbs such as chives, tarragon and parsley

1 One at a time, hold the crabs firmly and hit the underside with the heel of your hand. This should loosen the shell from the body. Using your thumbs, push against the body and pull away from the shell. Remove and discard the intestines and the grey gills.

2 Break off the claws and legs, then use a hammer or crackers to break them open. Using a pick, remove the meat from the claws and legs. Place the meat on a plate.

3 Using a skewer, pick out the white meat from the body cavities and place with the claw and leg meat, reserving a little white meat to garnish. Scoop out the brown meat from the shell and add to the rest of the crab meat.

4 Place the rice in a pan and add one-quarter of the stock. Bring to the boil and cook, stirring, until the liquid has been absorbed. Adding a ladleful of stock at a time, cook, stirring, until about two-thirds of the stock has been absorbed. Stir in the crab meat and herbs, and continue cooking, adding the remaining stock.

5 When the rice is almost cooked but still has some bite, remove it from the heat and adjust the seasoning. Cover and leave to stand for 3 minutes. Serve garnished with the reserved white crab meat.

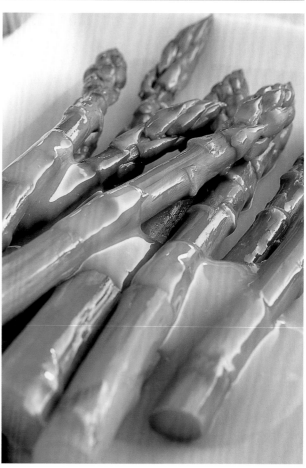

Vegetables and Side Dishes

A FEW CAREFULLY CHOSEN INGREDIENTS CAN BE BROUGHT

TOGETHER TO CREATE MOUTHWATERING SIDE DISHES

AND ACCOMPANIMENTS THAT WILL COMPLEMENT AND

ENHANCE ANY MAIN DISH. THIS COLLECTION OF TASTY

AND COLOURFUL COMBINATIONS OF VEGETABLES MAKES

HEALTHY EATING A TEMPTING TREAT.

Japanese-style Spinach with Toasted Sesame Seeds

This Japanese speciality, known as *O-hitashi*, has been served as a side dish on dining tables in Japan for centuries. Seasonal green vegetables are simply blanched and cooled and formed into little towers. With a little help from soy sauce and sesame seeds, they reveal their true flavour. Serve the spinach towers with simply cooked chicken or fish, such as salmon or tuna.

SERVES FOUR

1 Blanch the spinach leaves in lightly salted boiling water for 15 seconds. For Japanese-type spinach, hold the leafy part and slip the stems into the pan. After 15 seconds, drop in the leaves and cook for 20 seconds.

2 Drain immediately and place the spinach under running water. Squeeze out all the excess water by hand. Now what looked like a large amount of spinach has become a ball, roughly the size of an orange. Mix the shoyu and water, then pour on to the spinach. Mix well and leave to cool.

3 Meanwhile, put the sesame seeds in a dry frying pan and stir or toss until they start to pop. Remove from the heat and leave to cool.

4 Drain the spinach and squeeze out the excess sauce with your hands. Form the spinach into a log shape of about 4cm/1½in in diameter on a chopping board. Squeeze again to make it firm. With a sharp knife, cut it across into four cylinders.

5 Place the spinach cylinders on a large plate or individual dishes. Sprinkle with the toasted sesame seeds and a little salt and serve.

450g/1lb fresh young spinach

30ml/2 tbsp shoyu

30ml/2 tbsp water

15ml/1 tbsp sesame seeds

COOK'S TIP *Japanese spinach, the long-leaf type with the stalks and pink root intact, is best, but you can use ordinary young spinach leaves, or any soft and deep-green salad leaves – such as watercress, rocket (arugula) or lamb's lettuce.*

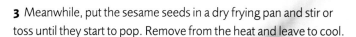

Braised Lettuce and Peas with Spring Onions

This light vegetable dish is based on the classic French method of braising peas with lettuce and spring onions in butter, and is delicious served with simply grilled fish or roast or grilled duck. A sprinkling of chopped fresh mint makes a fresh, flavoursome and extremely pretty garnish. Other legumes such as broad (fava) beans, mangetouts (snow peas) and sugar snaps can be used instead of peas to create a delicious variation.

SERVES FOUR

1 Melt half the butter in a wide, heavy pan over a low heat. Add the lettuces and spring onions.

2 Turn the vegetables in the butter, then sprinkle in salt and plenty of freshly ground black pepper. Cover, and cook the vegetables very gently for 5 minutes, stirring once.

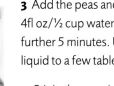

3 Add the peas and turn them in the buttery juices. Pour in 120ml/ 4fl oz/½ cup water, then cover and cook over a gentle heat for a further 5 minutes. Uncover and increase the heat to reduce the liquid to a few tablespoons.

4 Stir in the remaining butter and adjust the seasoning. Transfer to a warmed serving dish and serve immediately.

50g/2oz/¼ cup butter

4 Little Gem (Bibb) lettuces, halved lengthways

2 bunches spring onions (scallions), trimmed

400g/14oz shelled peas (about 1kg/2¼lb in pods)

EXTRAS

• Braise about 250g/ 9oz baby carrots with the lettuce.

• Cook 115g/4oz chopped smoked bacon or pancetta in the butter. Use one bunch of spring onions (scallions) and stir in some chopped parsley.

Asparagus with Lemon Sauce

Sometimes less is more: here a simple egg and lemon dressing brings out the best in asparagus. Serve the asparagus as an appetizer or side dish; alternatively, enjoy it for a light supper, with bread and butter to mop up the juices. When buying asparagus, look for bright coloured firm spears with tight buds – avoid those with tough woody stems. Choose roughly even-sized spears for uniform cooking.

SERVES FOUR

1 Cook the bundle of asparagus in a tall pan of lightly salted, boiling water for 7–10 minutes.

2 Drain well and arrange the asparagus in a serving dish. Reserve 200ml/7fl oz/scant 1 cup of the cooking liquid.

3 Blend the cornflour with the cooled, reserved cooking liquid and place in a small pan. Bring to the boil, stirring constantly, and cook over a gentle heat until the sauce thickens slightly. Remove the pan from the heat and leave to cool slightly.

4 Beat the egg yolks thoroughly with the lemon juice and gradually stir into the cooled sauce. Cook over a very low heat, stirring constantly, until the sauce is fairly thick. Be careful not to overheat the sauce or it may curdle. As soon as the sauce has thickened, remove the pan from the heat and continue stirring for 1 minute. Taste and season with salt. Leave the sauce to cool slightly.

5 Stir the cooled lemon sauce, then pour a little over the cooked asparagus. Cover and chill in the refrigerator for at least 2 hours before serving with the rest of the sauce to accompany.

675g/1½lb asparagus, tough ends removed, and tied in a bundle

15ml/1 tbsp cornflour (cornstarch)

2 egg yolks

juice of 1½ lemons

COOK'S TIP *For a slightly less tangy sauce, add a little caster (superfine) sugar with the salt in step 4.*

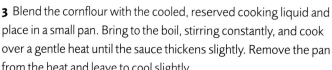

Caramelized Shallots

Sweet, golden shallots are good with all sorts of main dishes, including poultry or meat. Shallots have a less distinctive aroma than common onions and a milder flavour; they are also considered to be easier to digest. These caramelized shallots are also excellent with braised or roasted chestnuts, carrots or chunks of butternut squash. You may like to garnish the shallots with sprigs of fresh thyme before serving.

SERVES FOUR TO SIX

1 Heat the butter or oil in a large frying pan and add the shallots or onions in a single layer. Cook gently, turning occasionally, until they are lightly browned.

2 Sprinkle the sugar over the shallots and cook gently, turning the shallots in the juices, until the sugar begins to caramelize. Add the wine or port and let the mixture bubble for 4–5 minutes.

3 Add 150ml/¼ pint/⅔ cup water and seasoning. Cover and cook for 5 minutes, then remove the lid and cook until the liquid evaporates and the shallots are tender and glazed. Adjust the seasoning before serving.

50g/2oz/¼ cup butter or 60ml/4 tbsp olive oil

500g/1¼lb shallots or small onions, peeled with root ends intact

15ml/1 tbsp golden caster (superfine) sugar

30ml/2 tbsp red or white wine or port

Cauliflower with Garlic Crumbs

This simple dish makes a great accompaniment to any meat or fish dish. When buying cauliflower look for creamy white coloured florets with the inner green leaves curled round the flower. Discard cauliflowers with discoloured patches or yellow leaves. As an alternative, try using broccoli florets instead of the cauliflower. Broccoli should have a fresh appearance: avoid yellowing specimens and those that feel soft or are wilting.

SERVES FOUR TO SIX

1 Steam or boil the cauliflower in salted water until just tender. Drain and leave to cool.

2 Heat 60–75ml/4–5 tbsp of the olive or vegetable oil in a pan, add the breadcrumbs and cook over a medium heat, tossing and turning, until browned and crisp. Add the garlic, turn once or twice, then remove from the pan and set aside.

3 Heat the remaining oil in the pan, then add the cauliflower, mashing and breaking it up a little as it lightly browns in the oil. (Do not overcook but just cook until lightly browned.)

4 Add the garlic breadcrumbs to the pan and cook, stirring, until well combined, with some of the cauliflower still holding its shape. Season and serve hot or warm.

1 large cauliflower, cut into bitesize florets

90–120ml/6–8 tbsp olive or vegetable oil

130g/4½oz/2¼ cups dry white or wholemeal (whole-wheat) breadcrumbs

3–5 garlic cloves, thinly sliced or chopped

COOK'S TIP *Serve this wonderful, garlicky cauliflower dish as they do in Italy, with cooked pasta, such as spaghetti or rigatoni.*

Summer Squash and Baby New Potatoes in Warm Dill Sour Cream

Fresh vegetables and fragrant dill are delicious tossed in a simple sour cream or yogurt sauce. Choose small squash with bright skins that are free from blemishes and bruises. To make a simpler potato salad, pour the dill sour cream over warm cooked potatoes. Serve either version of the potato salad with poached salmon or chargrilled chicken.

SERVES FOUR

1 Cut the squash into pieces about the same size as the potatoes. Put the potatoes in a pan and add water to cover and a pinch of salt. Bring to the boil, then simmer for about 10 minutes, until almost tender. Add the squash and continue to cook until the vegetables are just tender, then drain.

2 Put the vegetables into a wide, shallow pan and gently stir in the finely chopped fresh dill and chives.

3 Remove the pan from the heat and stir in the sour cream or yogurt. Return to the heat and heat gently until warm. Season and serve.

400g/14oz mixed squash, such as yellow and green courgettes (zucchini), and pale green patty pan

400g/14oz tiny, baby new potatoes

1 large handful mixed fresh dill and chives, finely chopped

300ml/½ pint/1¼ cups sour cream or Greek (US strained plain) yogurt

Baked Winter Squash with Tomatoes

Acorn, butternut or Hubbard squash can all be used in this simple recipe. Serve the squash as a light main course, with warm crusty bread, or as a side dish for grilled meat or poultry. Canned chopped tomatoes with herbs are used in this recipe. A variety of flavoured canned tomatoes are now available including garlic, onion and olive – they are ideal for adding a combination of flavours when time is short.

SERVES FOUR TO SIX

1 Preheat the oven to 160°C/325°F/Gas 3. Heat the oil in a pan and cook the pumpkin or squash slices, in batches, until golden brown, removing them from the pan as they are cooked.

2 Add the tomatoes and cook over a medium-high heat until the mixture is of a sauce consistency. Stir in the rosemary and season to taste with salt and pepper.

3 Layer the pumpkin slices and tomatoes in an ovenproof dish, ending with a layer of tomatoes. Bake for 35 minutes, or until the top is lightly glazed and beginning to turn golden brown, and the pumpkin is tender. Serve immediately.

45ml/3 tbsp garlic-flavoured olive oil

1kg/2¼lb pumpkin or orange winter squash, peeled and sliced

2 x 400g/14oz cans chopped tomatoes with herbs

2–3 fresh rosemary sprigs, stems removed and leaves chopped

Stewed Okra with Tomatoes and Coriander

This is a favourite Middle-Eastern way to prepare okra. Add wedges of lemon as a garnish so that their juice can be squeezed over the vegetables to taste. Okra, also known as lady's fingers, are narrow green lantern-shaped pods. They contain a row of seeds that ooze a viscous liquid when cooked. This liquid acts as a natural thickener in a variety of curries and soups.

SERVES FOUR TO SIX

1 Heat the tomatoes and the cinnamon, cumin and cloves with half the coriander in a pan, then season to taste with salt and freshly ground black pepper and bring to the boil.

2 Add the okra and cook, stirring constantly, for 1–2 minutes. Reduce the heat to low, then simmer, stirring occasionally, for 20–30 minutes, until the okra is tender.

3 Taste for spicing and seasoning, and adjust if necessary, adding more of any one spice, salt or pepper to taste. Stir in the remaining coriander. Serve hot, warm or cold.

400g/14oz can chopped tomatoes with onions and garlic

generous pinch each of ground cinnamon, cumin and cloves

90ml/6 tbsp chopped fresh coriander (cilantro) leaves

800g/1¾lb okra

Tomato and Aubergine Gratin

This colourful, Mediterranean dish makes the perfect partner to grilled, pan-fried or baked meat or poultry. If you prefer, thinly sliced courgettes (zucchini) can be used in this dish instead of the aubergines. Grill the courgettes for 10–15 minutes. Choose plum tomatoes if you can – they have fewer seeds than most round tomatoes, so are less watery and are ideal for cooking.

SERVES FOUR TO SIX

1 Preheat the grill (broiler). Thinly slice the aubergines and arrange them in a single layer on a foil-lined grill rack. Brush the aubergine slices with some of the olive oil and grill (broil) for 15–20 minutes, turning once, until golden on both sides. Brush the second side with more olive oil after turning the slices.

2 Preheat the oven to 200°C/400°F/Gas 6. Toss the aubergine and tomato slices together in a bowl with a little seasoning, then pile them into a shallow, ovenproof dish. Drizzle with any remaining olive oil and sprinkle with the grated Parmesan cheese. Bake for 20 minutes, until the cheese is golden and the vegetables are hot. Serve the gratin immediately.

2 medium aubergines (eggplant), about 500g/1¼ lb

90ml/6 tbsp olive oil

400g/14oz ripe tomatoes, sliced

40g/1½oz/½ cup freshly grated Parmesan cheese

Deep-fried Artichokes

This is an Italian speciality, named *carciofi alla giudia*. The artichokes are baked, then pressed to open them and plunged into hot oil, where their leaves twist and brown, turning the artichokes into crispy flowers. Serve with lamb or pork steaks.

SERVES FOUR

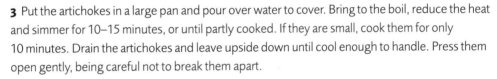

2–3 lemons, halved

4–8 small young globe artichokes

olive or vegetable oil, for deep-frying

1 Fill a large bowl with cold water and stir in the juice of one or two of the lemons. Trim and discard the stems of the artichokes, then trim off their tough ends and remove all the tough outer leaves until you reach the pale pointed centre. Carefully open the leaves of one of the artichokes by pressing it against the table or poking them open. Trim the tops if they are sharp.

2 If there is any choke inside the artichoke, remove it with a melon baller or small pointed spoon. Put the artichoke in the acidulated water and prepare the remaining artichokes in the same way.

3 Put the artichokes in a large pan and pour over water to cover. Bring to the boil, reduce the heat and simmer for 10–15 minutes, or until partly cooked. If they are small, cook them for only 10 minutes. Drain the artichokes and leave upside down until cool enough to handle. Press them open gently, being careful not to break them apart.

4 Fill a pan with oil to a depth of 5–7.5cm/2–3in and heat. Add one or two artichokes at a time, with the leaves uppermost, and press down with a spoon to open up the leaves. Fry for 5–8 minutes, turning, until golden and crisp. Remove from the pan, and drain on kitchen paper. Serve immediately, with the remaining lemon cut into wedges.

COOK'S TIP *Select immature artichokes, before their chokes have formed. If you like, you can prepare and boil them ahead and deep-fry just before serving.*

133

Leek Fritters

These crispy fried morsels are best served at room temperature, with a good squeeze of lemon juice and a sprinkling of salt and freshly grated nutmeg. Matzo meal, a traditional Jewish ingredient, is used in these fritters: it is made from crumbled matzo, an unleavened bread, similar to water biscuits. Matzo meal is used in a similar way to breadcrumbs, which can also be used to make these fritters.

SERVES FOUR

1 Cook the leeks in salted boiling water for 5 minutes, or until just tender and bright green. Drain well and leave to cool.

2 Chop the leeks coarsely. Put in a bowl and combine with the matzo meal, eggs and seasoning.

3 Heat 5mm/¼in oil in a frying pan. Using two tablespoons, carefully spoon the leek mixture into the hot oil. Cook over a medium-high heat until golden brown on the underside, then turn and cook the second side. Drain on kitchen paper. Add more oil if needed and heat before cooking more mixture.

4 large leeks, total weight about 1kg/ 2¼ lb, thickly sliced

120–175ml/ 4–6fl oz/½–¾ cup coarse matzo meal

2 eggs, lightly beaten

olive or vegetable oil, for shallow frying

Bubble and Squeak

Whether you have leftovers or cook this old-fashioned classic from fresh, be sure to give it a really good "squeak" in the pan so it turns a rich honey brown. Serve as an accompaniment to grilled pork chops or fried eggs, or simply serve with warm bread for a quick supper. If you prefer, cook the bubble and squeak in individual-sized portions – divide into four and form into patties before cooking.

SERVES FOUR

1 Heat 30ml/2 tbsp of the bacon fat or oil in a heavy frying pan. Add the onion and cook over a medium heat, stirring frequently, until softened but not browned.

2 In a large bowl, mix together the potatoes and cooked cabbage or sprouts and season with salt and plenty of pepper to taste.

3 Add the vegetables to the pan with the cooked onions, stir well, then press the vegetable mixture into a large, even cake.

4 Cook over a medium heat for about 15 minutes, until the cake is browned underneath.

5 Invert a large plate over the pan, and, holding it tightly against the pan, turn them both over together. Lift off the frying pan, return it to the heat and add the remaining bacon fat or oil. When hot, slide the cake back into the pan, browned side uppermost.

6 Cook over a medium heat for 10 minutes, or until the underside is golden brown. Serve hot, in wedges.

60ml/4 tbsp bacon fat or vegetable oil

1 medium onion, finely chopped

450g/1lb floury potatoes, cooked and mashed

225g/8oz cooked cabbage or Brussels sprouts, finely chopped

EXTRAS *When made with vegetables from a roast dinner, the mixture can be moistened with leftover gravy, making it bubble as it cooks and giving a really delicious savoury flavour.*

Fennel, Potato and Garlic Mash

This flavoursome mash of potato, fennel and garlic goes well with practically all main dishes, whether fish, poultry or meat. Floury varieties of potato such as Pentland Squire, King Edward or Marfona are best for mashing as they produce a light fluffy result. Waxy potatoes are more suitable for baking, or for salads, as they produce a dense, rather starchy mash.

SERVES FOUR

1 Boil the potatoes in salted water for 20 minutes, until tender.

2 Meanwhile, trim and coarsely chop the fennel, reserving any feathery tops. Chop the tops and set them aside. Heat 30ml/2 tbsp of the oil in a heavy pan. Add the fennel, cover and cook over a low heat for 20–30 minutes, until soft but not browned.

3 Drain and mash the potatoes. Purée the fennel in a food mill or blender and beat it into the potato with the remaining oil.

4 Warm the milk or cream and beat sufficient into the potato and fennel to make a creamy, light mixture. Season to taste and reheat gently, then beat in any chopped fennel tops. Serve immediately.

800g/1¾lb potatoes, cut into chunks

2 large fennel bulbs

90ml/6 tbsp garlic-flavoured olive oil

120–150ml/4–5fl oz/ ½–⅔ cup milk or single (light) cream

Champ

This traditional Irish dish of potatoes and green or spring onions is enriched with a wickedly indulgent amount of butter – for complete indulgence, replace 60ml/4 tbsp of the milk with crème fraîche or buttermilk. Serve the champ as an accompaniment to beef or lamb stew for a warming and hearty winter meal.

SERVES FOUR

**1kg/2¼lb potatoes,
cut into chunks**

300ml/½ pint/1¼ cups milk

**1 bunch spring onions (scallions),
thinly sliced, plus extra to garnish**

**115g/4oz/½ cup slightly
salted butter**

1 Boil the potatoes in lightly salted water for 20–25 minutes, or until they are tender. Drain and mash the potatoes with a fork until smooth.

2 Place the milk, spring onions and half the butter in a small pan and set over a low heat until just simmering. Cook for 2–3 minutes, until the butter has melted and the spring onions have softened.

3 Beat the milk mixture into the mashed potato using a wooden spoon until the mixture is light and fluffy. Reheat gently, adding seasoning to taste.

4 Turn the potato into a warmed serving dish and make a well in the centre with a spoon. Place the remaining butter in the well and let it melt. Serve immediately, sprinkled with extra spring onion.

EXTRAS

To make colcannon, another Irish speciality, follow the main recipe, using half the butter. Cook about 500g/1¼lb finely shredded green cabbage or kale in a little water until just tender, drain thoroughly and then beat into the creamed potato. This is delicious served with sausages and grilled (broiled) ham or bacon. The colcannon may also be fried in butter and then browned under the grill (broiler).

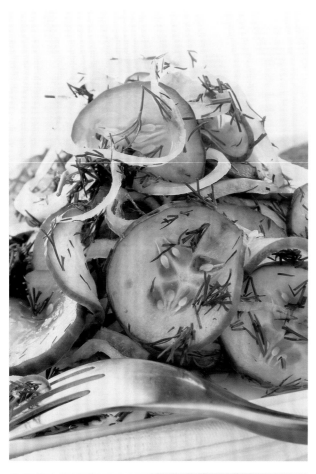

Salads

WHETHER SERVED AS A MAIN COURSE OR AN
ACCOMPANIMENT, SALADS ARE ALWAYS A REFRESHING
AND WELCOME CHANGE. THE MOST SUCCESSFUL ARE
COMPOSED OF ONLY A FEW INGREDIENTS – COOKED OR
RAW – WHOSE COLOURS, TEXTURES AND FLAVOURS
COMPLEMENT AND BALANCE PERFECTLY.

Sour Cucumber with Fresh Dill

This is half pickle, half salad, and totally delicious served with pumpernickel or other coarse, dark, full-flavoured bread, as a light meal or an appetizer. Choose smooth-skinned, smallish cucumbers for this recipe as larger ones tend to be less tender, with tough skins and bitter indigestible seeds. If you can only buy a large cucumber, peel it before slicing.

SERVES FOUR

1 In a large mixing bowl, combine together the thinly sliced cucumbers and the thinly sliced onion. Season the vegetables with salt and toss together until they are thoroughly combined. Leave the mixture to stand in a cool place for 5–10 minutes.

2 Add the cider vinegar, 30–45ml/2–3 tbsp water and the chopped fresh dill to the cucumber and onion mixture. Toss all the ingredients together until well combined, then chill in the refrigerator for a few hours, or until ready to serve.

2 small cucumbers, thinly sliced

3 onions, thinly sliced

75–90ml/5–6 tbsp cider vinegar

30–45ml/2–3 tbsp chopped fresh dill

EXTRAS

For a sweet and sour mixture, add 45ml/3 tbsp caster (superfine) sugar with the cider vinegar in step 2.

Beetroot with Fresh Mint

This simple and decorative beetroot salad can be served as part of a selection of salads, as an appetizer, or as an accompaniment to grilled or roasted pork or lamb. Balsamic vinegar is a rich, dark vinegar with a mellow, deep flavour. It can be used to dress a variety of salad ingredients and is particularly good drizzled over a tomato and basil salad.

SERVES FOUR

1 Slice the beetroot or cut into even-size dice with a sharp knife. Put the beetroot in a bowl. Add the balsamic vinegar, olive oil and a pinch of salt and toss together to combine.

2 Add half the thinly shredded fresh mint to the salad and toss lightly until thoroughly combined. Place the salad in the refrigerator and chill for about 1 hour. Serve garnished with the remaining thinly shredded mint leaves.

4–6 cooked beetroot (beet)

15–30ml/1–2 tbsp balsamic vinegar

30ml/2 tbsp olive oil

1 bunch fresh mint, leaves stripped and thinly shredded

EXTRAS

To make Tunisian beetroot, add a little harissa to taste and substitute chopped fresh coriander (cilantro) for the shredded mint.

Globe Artichokes with Green Beans and Garlic Dressing

Piquant garlic dressing or creamy aioli go perfectly with these lightly-cooked vegetables. Serve lemon wedges with the artichokes so that their juice may be squeezed over to taste. The vegetables can also be garnished with finely shredded lemon rind. Artichokes should feel heavy for their size – make sure that the inner leaves are wrapped tightly round the choke and the heart inside.

SERVES FOUR TO SIX

225g/8oz green beans

3 small globe artichokes

15ml/1 tbsp lemon-flavoured olive oil

250ml/8fl oz/1 cup garlic dressing or aioli

1 Cook the beans in boiling water for 1–2 minutes, until slightly softened. Drain well.

2 Trim the artichoke stalks close to the base. Cook them in a large pan of salted water for about 30 minutes, or until you can easily pull away a leaf from the base. Drain well.

3 Using a sharp knife, halve them lengthways and ease out their chokes using a teaspoon.

4 Arrange the artichokes and beans on serving plates and drizzle with the oil. Season with coarse salt and a little pepper. Spoon the garlic dressing or aioli into the hearts and serve warm.

5 To eat the artichokes, pull the leaves from the base one at a time and use to scoop a little of the dressing. It is only the fleshy end of each leaf that is eaten as well as the base, bottom or "fond".

Halloumi and Grape Salad

Firm and salty halloumi cheese is a great standby ingredient for turning a simple salad into a special dish. In this recipe it is tossed with sweet, juicy grapes, which complement its flavour and texture. Fresh young thyme leaves and dill taste especially good mixed with the salad. Serve with a crusty walnut or sun-dried tomato bread for a light lunch.

SERVES FOUR

1 Toss together the salad leaves and fresh herb sprigs and the green and black grapes, then transfer to a large serving plate.

2 Thinly slice the halloumi cheese. Heat a large non-stick frying pan. Add the sliced halloumi cheese and cook briefly until it just starts to turn golden brown on the underside. Turn the cheese with a fish slice or metal spatula and cook the other side until it is golden brown.

3 Arrange the fried cheese over the salad on the plate. Pour over the oil and lemon juice or vinegar dressing and serve immediately while the cheese is still hot.

150g/5oz mixed salad leaves and tender fresh herb sprigs

175g/6oz mixed seedless green and black grapes

250g/9oz halloumi cheese

75ml/5 tbsp oil and lemon juice or vinegar dressing

Watermelon and Feta Salad

The combination of sweet watermelon with salty feta cheese is inspired by Turkish tradition. The salad may be served plain and light, on a leafy base, or with a herbed vinaigrette dressing drizzled over. It is perfect served as an appetizer. Feta cheese is salty because it is preserved in brine – but the salt is not supposed to overpower the taste of the cheese.

SERVES FOUR

4 slices watermelon, chilled

130g/4½oz feta cheese, preferably sheep's milk feta, cut into bitesize pieces

handful of mixed seeds, such as lightly toasted pumpkin seeds and sunflower seeds

10–15 black olives

1 Cut the rind off the watermelon and remove as many seeds as possible. Cut the flesh into triangular-shaped chunks.

2 Mix the watermelon, feta cheese, mixed seeds and black olives. Cover and chill the salad for 30 minutes before serving.

COOK'S TIP *The best choice of olives for this recipe are plump black Mediterranean ones, such as kalamata, other shiny, brined varieties or dry-cured black olives.*

Tomato, Bean and Fried Basil Salad

Infusing basil in hot oil brings out its wonderful, aromatic flavour, which works so well in almost any tomato dish. Various canned beans or chickpeas can be used instead of mixed beans in this simple dish, as they all taste good and make a wholesome salad to serve as an accompaniment or a satisfying snack with some warm, grainy bread.

SERVES FOUR

1 Reserve one-third of the basil leaves for garnish, then tear the remainder into pieces. Pour the olive oil into a small pan. Add the torn basil and heat gently for 1 minute, until the basil sizzles and begins to colour.

2 Place the halved cherry tomatoes and beans in a bowl. Pour in the basil oil and add a little salt and plenty of freshly ground black pepper. Toss the ingredients together gently, cover and leave to marinate at room temperature for at least 30 minutes. Serve the salad sprinkled with the remaining basil leaves.

15g/½oz/½ cup fresh basil leaves

75ml/5 tbsp extra virgin olive oil

300g/11oz cherry tomatoes, halved

400g/14oz can mixed beans, drained and rinsed

Moroccan Date, Orange and Carrot Salad

Take exotic fresh dates and marry them with everyday ingredients, such as carrots and oranges, to make this deliciously different salad. The salad looks really pretty arranged on a base of sweet Little Gem (Bibb) lettuce leaves. This fruity salad is excellent served with chargrilled lamb steaks, or with skewered lamb.

SERVES FOUR

3 carrots

3 oranges

115g/4oz fresh dates, stoned (pitted) and cut lengthways into eighths

25g/1oz/¼ cup toasted whole almonds, chopped

1 Grate the carrots and place in a mound in a serving dish, or on four individual plates.

2 Peel and segment two of the oranges and arrange the orange segments around the carrot. Season with salt and freshly ground black pepper. Pile the dates on top, then sprinkle with the chopped, toasted almonds.

3 Squeeze the juice from the remaining orange and sprinkle it over the salad. Chill in the refrigerator for an hour before serving.

Pink Grapefruit and Avocado Salad

Smooth, creamy avocado and zesty citrus fruit are perfect partners in an attractive, refreshing salad. Pink grapefruit are tangy but not too sharp, or try large oranges for a sweeter flavour. Avocados turn brown quickly when exposed to the air: the acidic grapefruit juice will prevent this from occurring, so combine the ingredients as soon as the avocados have been sliced.

SERVES FOUR

1 Slice the top and bottom off a grapefruit, then cut off all the peel and pith from around the side. Working over a small bowl to catch the juices, cut out the segments from between the membranes and place them in a separate bowl. Squeeze any juices remaining in the membranes into the bowl, then discard them. Repeat with the remaining grapefruit.

2 Halve, stone (pit) and peel the avocados. Slice the flesh and add it to the grapefruit segments. Whisk a little salt and then the chilli oil into the grapefruit juice.

3 Pile the rocket leaves on to four serving plates and top with the grapefruit segments and avocado. Pour over the dressing and serve. Alternatively, toss the rocket with the grapefruit, avocado and dressing, then divide the salad among plates or bowls.

2 pink grapefruit

2 ripe avocados

30ml/2 tbsp chilli oil

**90g/3½oz
rocket (arugula)**

Turnip Salad in Sour Cream

Usually served cooked, raw young tender turnips have a tangy, slightly peppery flavour. Serve this as an accompaniment for grilled poultry or meat. It is also delicious as a light appetizer, garnished with parsley and paprika, and served with warmed flat breads such as pitta or naan. Garnish the salad with fresh flat leaf parsley and paprika, if you like.

SERVES FOUR

1 Thinly slice or coarsely grate the turnips. Alternatively, thinly slice half the turnips and grate the remaining half. Put in a bowl.

2 Add the onion and vinegar and season to taste with salt and plenty of freshly ground black pepper. Toss together, then stir in the sour cream. Chill well before serving.

VARIATIONS *Large white radishes can be used instead of turnips and crème fraîche can be substituted for the sour cream. The salad is good with a selection of salads and cold dishes for a light lunch or long and leisurely supper.*

2–4 young, tender turnips, peeled

¼–½ onion, finely chopped

2–3 drops white wine vinegar, or to taste

60–90ml/4–6 tbsp sour cream

Moroccan Carrot Salad

In this intriguing salad from North Africa, the carrots are lightly cooked before being tossed in a cumin and coriander vinaigrette. Cumin is widely used in Indian and Mexican cooking, as well as North African cuisines. It has a strong and spicy aroma and a warm pungent flavour that goes particularly well with root vegetables. This salad is a perfect accompaniment for both everyday or special meals.

SERVES FOUR TO SIX

3–4 carrots, thinly sliced

1.5ml/¼ tsp ground cumin, or to taste

60ml/4 tbsp garlic-flavoured oil and vinegar dressing

30ml/2 tbsp chopped fresh coriander (cilantro) leaves or a mixture of coriander and parsley

1 Cook the thinly sliced carrots by either steaming or boiling in lightly salted water until they are just tender but not soft. Drain the carrots, leave for a few minutes to dry and cool, then put into a mixing bowl.

2 Add the cumin, garlic dressing and herbs. Season to taste and chill well before serving. Check the seasoning just before serving and add more ground cumin, salt or black pepper, if required.

Warm Chorizo and Spinach Salad

Spanish chorizo sausage contributes an intense spiciness to any ingredient with which it is cooked. In this hearty warm salad, spinach has sufficient flavour to compete with the chorizo. Watercress or rocket (arugula) could be used instead of the spinach, if you prefer. For an added dimension use a flavoured olive oil – rosemary, garlic or chilli oil would work perfectly. Serve the salad with warm crusty bread to soak up all the delicious cooking juices.

SERVES FOUR

1 Discard any tough stalks from the spinach. Pour the oil into a large frying pan and add the sausage. Cook gently for 3 minutes, until the sausage slices start to shrivel slightly and colour.

2 Add the spinach leaves and remove the pan from the heat. Toss the spinach in the warm oil until it just starts to wilt. Add the sherry vinegar and a little seasoning. Toss the ingredients briefly, then serve immediately, while still warm.

225g/8oz baby spinach leaves

90ml/6 tbsp extra virgin olive oil

150g/5oz chorizo sausage, very thinly sliced

30ml/2 tbsp sherry vinegar

Potato and Olive Salad

This delicious salad is simple and zesty – the perfect choice for lunch, as an accompaniment, or as an appetizer. Similar in appearance to flat leaf parsley, fresh coriander has a distinctive pungent, almost spicy flavour. It is widely used in India, the Middle and Far East and in eastern Mediterranean countries. This potato salad is particularly good served as part of a brunch.

SERVES FOUR

8 large new potatoes

45–60ml/3–4 tbsp garlic-flavoured oil and vinegar dressing

60–90ml/4–6 tbsp chopped fresh herbs, such as coriander (cilantro) and chives

10–15 dry-fleshed black Mediterranean olives

1 Cut the new potatoes into chunks. Put them in a pan, pour in water to cover and add a pinch of salt. Bring to the boil, then reduce the heat and cook gently for about 10 minutes, or until the potatoes are just tender. Drain well and leave in a colander to dry thoroughly and cool slightly.

2 When they are cool enough to handle, chop the potatoes and put them in a serving bowl.

3 Drizzle the garlic dressing over the potatoes. Toss well and sprinkle with the chopped fresh coriander and chives, and black olives. Chill in the refrigerator for at least 1 hour before serving.

EXTRAS *Add a pinch of ground cumin or a sprinkling of roasted whole cumin seeds to spice up the salad.*

Asparagus, Bacon and Leaf Salad

This excellent salad turns a plain roast chicken or simple grilled fish into an interesting meal, especially when served with buttered new potatoes. It also makes an appetizing first course or light lunch. A wide range of different salad leaves are readily available – frisée has feathery, curly, slightly bitter tasting leaves and is a member of the chicory family. Frisée leaves range in colour from yellow-white to yellow-green.

SERVES FOUR

1 Trim off any tough stalk ends from the asparagus and cut the spears into three, setting the tender tips aside. Heat a 1cm/½in depth of water in a frying pan until simmering. Reserve the asparagus tips and cook the remainder of the spears in the water for about 3 minutes, until almost tender. Add the tips and cook for 1 minute more. Drain and refresh under cold, running water.

2 Dry-fry the bacon until golden and crisp and then set it aside to cool slightly. Use kitchen scissors to snip it into bitesize pieces. Place the frisée or mixed leaf salad in a bowl and add the bacon.

3 Add the asparagus and a little black pepper to the salad. Pour the dressing over and toss the salad lightly, then serve before the leaves begin to wilt.

500g/1¼lb medium asparagus spears

130g/4½oz thin-cut smoked back (lean) bacon

250g/9oz frisée lettuce leaves or mixed leaf salad

100ml/3½fl oz/ scant ½ cup French dressing

Anchovy and Roasted Pepper Salad

Sweet peppers, salty anchovies and plenty of garlic make an intensely flavoured salad that is delicious with meat, poultry or cheese. It also makes a tasty snack with olive bread. If you find that canned anchovies are too salty for your liking, you can reduce their saltiness by soaking them in milk for 20 minutes. Drain off the oil first and after soaking drain and rinse them in cold water.

SERVES FOUR

2 red, 2 orange and 2 yellow (bell) peppers, halved and seeded

50g/2oz can anchovies in olive oil

2 garlic cloves

45ml/3 tbsp balsamic vinegar

1 Preheat the oven to 200°C/400°F/Gas 6. Place the peppers, cut side down, in a roasting pan. Roast for 30-40 minutes, until the skins are charred. Transfer the peppers to a bowl, cover with clear film (plastic wrap) and leave for 15 minutes.

2 Peel the peppers, then cut them into chunky strips. Drain the anchovies and halve the fillets lengthways.

3 Slice the garlic as thinly as possible and place it in a large bowl. Stir in the olive oil, vinegar and a little pepper. Add the peppers and anchovies and use a spoon and fork to fold the ingredients together. Cover and chill until ready to serve.

Ice Creams and Frozen Desserts

ICE CREAMS AND ICED DESSERTS CAN MAKE A PERFECT,

REFRESHING END TO A MEAL. HOME-MADE ICES, WHETHER

A LIGHTLY PERFUMED SORBET, A CREAMY KULFI OR A RICH

AND CREAMY ICE CREAM GÂTEAU, ARE SURPRISINGLY

EASY TO MAKE AND A WONDERFUL TREAT TO SERVE

TO GUESTS AND FAMILY ALIKE.

Lemon Sorbet

This is probably the most classic sorbet of all. Refreshingly tangy and yet deliciously smooth, it quite literally melts in the mouth. Try to buy unwaxed lemons for recipes such as this one where the lemon rind is used. The wax coating can adversely affect the flavour of the rind.

SERVES SIX

200g/7oz/1 cup caster (superfine) sugar, plus extra for coating rind to decorate

4 lemons, well scrubbed

1 egg white

1 Put the sugar in a pan and pour in 300ml/½ pint/1¼ cups water. Bring to the boil, stirring occasionally until the sugar has just dissolved.

2 Using a swivel vegetable peeler, pare the rind thinly from two of the lemons so that it falls straight into the pan.

3 Simmer for 2 minutes without stirring, then take the pan off the heat. Leave to cool, then chill.

4 Squeeze the juice from all the lemons and add it to the syrup. Strain the syrup into a shallow freezerproof container, reserving the rind. Freeze the mixture for 4 hours, until it is mushy.

5 Process the sorbet (sherbet) in a food processor until it is smooth. Lightly whisk the egg white with a fork until it is just frothy. Replace the sorbet in the container, beat in the egg white and return the mixture to the freezer for 4 hours, or until it is firm.

6 Cut the reserved lemon rind into fine shreds and cook them in boiling water for 5 minutes, or until tender. Drain, then place on a plate and sprinkle generously with caster sugar. Scoop the sorbet into bowls or glasses and decorate with the sugared lemon rind.

Strawberry and Lavender Sorbet

A hint of lavender transforms a familiar strawberry sorbet into a perfumed dinner-party dessert. When buying strawberries look for plump, shiny fruit without any signs of straining or leakage at the bottom of the punnet – this suggests that the fruit at the bottom has been squashed. To hull strawberries, prise out the leafy top with a sharp knife or a specially designed strawberry huller.

SERVES SIX

1 Place the sugar in a pan and pour in 300ml/½ pint/1¼ cups water. Bring to the boil, stirring until the sugar has dissolved.

2 Take the pan off the heat, add the lavender flowers and leave to infuse (steep) for 1 hour. If time permits, chill the syrup in the refrigerator before using.

3 Process the strawberries in a food processor or in batches in a blender, then press the purée through a large sieve into a bowl.

4 Pour the purée into a freezerproof container, strain in the syrup and freeze for 4 hours, or until mushy. Transfer to a food processor and process until smooth. Whisk the egg white until frothy, and stir into the sorbet (sherbet). Spoon the sorbet back into the container and freeze until firm.

5 Serve in scoops, piled into tall glasses, and decorate with sprigs of lavender flowers.

150g/5oz/¾ cup caster (superfine) sugar

6 fresh lavender flowers, plus extra to decorate

500g/1¼lb/5 cups strawberries, hulled

1 egg white

Blackcurrant Sorbet

Wonderfully sharp and bursting with flavour, blackcurrants make a really fabulous sorbet. Blackcurrants are more acidic than white or redcurrants and are very rarely eaten raw. Taste the mixture after adding the syrup, and if you find it a little too tart, add a little more sugar before freezing.

500g/1¼lb/5 cups blackcurrants, trimmed, plus extra to decorate

150g/5oz/¾ cup caster (superfine) sugar

1 egg white

SERVES SIX

1 Put the blackcurrants in a pan and add 150ml/¼ pint/⅔ cup water. Cover the pan and simmer for 5 minutes, or until the fruit is soft. Cool, then process to a purée in a food processor or blender.

2 Set a large sieve over a bowl, pour the purée into the sieve, then press it through the mesh with the back of a spoon to form a smooth liquid.

3 Pour 200ml/7fl oz/scant 1 cup water into a clean pan. Add the sugar and bring to the boil, stirring until the sugar has dissolved. Pour the syrup into a bowl. Cool, then chill.

4 Mix the blackcurrant purée and sugar syrup together. Spoon into a freezerproof container and freeze until mushy. Lightly whisk the egg white until just frothy. Process the sorbet (sherbet) in a food processor until smooth, then return it to the container and stir in the egg white. Freeze for 4 hours, or until firm.

5 Transfer the sorbet to the refrigerator about 15 minutes before serving. Serve in scoops, decorated with the blackcurrant sprigs.

Damson Water Ice

Perfectly ripe damsons are sharp and full of flavour – if you can't find damsons, use another deep-red variety of plum or extra-juicy Victoria plums. To add an extra, nutty flavour to this mouthwatering ice, serve sprinkled with finely chopped toasted almonds.

SERVES SIX

500g/1¼lb ripe damsons, washed

150g/5oz/¾ cup caster (superfine) sugar

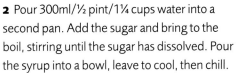

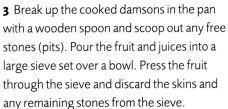

1 Put the damsons into a pan and add 150ml/¼ pint/⅔ cup water. Cover and simmer gently for 10 minutes, or until the damsons are tender.

2 Pour 300ml/½ pint/1¼ cups water into a second pan. Add the sugar and bring to the boil, stirring until the sugar has dissolved. Pour the syrup into a bowl, leave to cool, then chill.

3 Break up the cooked damsons in the pan with a wooden spoon and scoop out any free stones (pits). Pour the fruit and juices into a large sieve set over a bowl. Press the fruit through the sieve and discard the skins and any remaining stones from the sieve.

4 Pour the damson purée into a shallow plastic container. Stir in the syrup and freeze for 6 hours, beating once or twice to break up the ice crystals.

5 Spoon into tall serving glasses or dishes and serve the water ice with wafers.

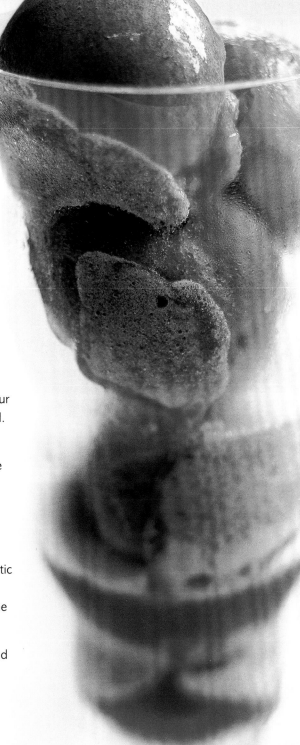

VARIATION Apricot water ice can be made in exactly the same way. Flavour the water ice with a little lemon or orange rind or add a broken cinnamon stick to the pan when poaching the fruit. Serve garnished with sprigs of mint or nasturtium flowers.

Peach and Cardamom Yogurt Ice

Make the most of spices that are familiar in savoury cooking by discovering their potential for sweet dishes. Cardamom, often used in Indian cooking, has a warm pungent aroma and a subtle lemon flavour. Although it is made with yogurt rather than cream, this ice cream has a luxurious velvety texture and it is a healthy choice, too.

SERVES FOUR

8 cardamom pods

6 peaches, total weight about 500g/1¼lb, halved and stoned (pitted)

75g/3oz/6 tbsp caster (superfine) sugar

200ml/7fl oz/scant 1 cup natural (plain) yogurt

1 Put the cardamom pods on a board and crush them with the base of a ramekin, or place in a mortar and crush with a pestle.

2 Chop the peaches coarsely and put them in a pan. Add the crushed cardamom pods, with their black seeds, the sugar and 30ml/2 tbsp water. Cover and simmer for 10 minutes, or until the fruit is tender. Leave to cool.

3 Process the peach mixture in a food processor or blender until smooth, then press through a sieve placed over a bowl.

4 Mix the yogurt into the sieved purée and pour into a freezerproof container. Freeze for 5–6 hours, until firm, beating once or twice with a fork, electric whisk, or in a processor to break up the ice crystals.

5 Scoop the ice cream on to a large platter and serve.

Blackberry Ice Cream

There could scarcely be fewer ingredients in this delicious, vibrant ice cream, which is simple to make and ideal as a prepare-ahead dessert. Serve the ice cream with biscuits (cookies), such as shortbread or almond biscuits, to provide a delicious contrast in taste and texture.

SERVES FOUR TO SIX

500g/1¼lb/5 cups blackberries, hulled, plus extra to decorate

75g/3oz/6 tbsp caster (superfine) sugar

300ml/½ pint/1¼ cups whipping cream

crisp dessert biscuits (cookies), to serve

COOK'S TIP

Frozen blackberries can be used instead of fresh. You will need to increase the cooking time to 10 minutes and stir occasionally.

1 Put the blackberries into a pan, add 30ml/2 tbsp water and the sugar. Cover and simmer for 5 minutes, until just soft.

2 Tip the fruit into a sieve placed over a bowl and press it through the mesh, using a wooden spoon. Leave to cool, then chill.

3 Whip the cream until it is just thick but still soft enough to fall from a spoon, then mix it with the chilled fruit purée. Pour the mixture into a freezerproof container and freeze for 2 hours, or until it is part frozen.

4 Mash the mixture with a fork or process it in a food processor to break up the ice crystals. Return it to the freezer for 4 hours more, mashing or processing the mixture again after 2 hours.

5 Scoop the ice cream into dishes and decorate with extra blackberries. Serve with crisp dessert biscuits.

Kulfi

This favourite Indian ice cream is traditionally made by carefully boiling milk until it has reduced to about one-third of its original quantity. Although you can save time by using condensed milk, nothing beats the luscious result achieved by using the authentic method. When they are available, rose petals are a stylish decoration in addition to the pistachio nuts.

SERVES FOUR

1.5 litres/2½ pints/6¼ cups full-fat (whole) milk

3 cardamom pods

25g/1oz/2 tbsp caster (superfine) sugar

50g/2oz/½ cup pistachio nuts, skinned

1 Pour the milk into a large, heavy pan. Bring to the boil, reduce the heat and simmer gently for 1 hour, stirring occasionally.

2 Put the cardamom pods in a mortar and crush them with a pestle. Add the pods and the seeds to the milk and continue to simmer, stirring frequently, for 1–1½ hours, or until the milk has reduced to about 475ml/16fl oz/2 cups. Strain the milk into a jug (pitcher), stir in the sugar and leave to cool.

3 Grind half the pistachios in a blender or nut grinder. Cut the remaining pistachios into thin slivers and set them aside for decoration. Stir the ground nuts into the milk mixture.

4 Pour the milk and pistachio mixture into four kulfi or lolly (popsicle) moulds. Freeze the mixture overnight or until firm.

5 To unmould the kulfi, half fill a plastic container or bowl with very hot water, stand the moulds in the water and count to ten. Immediately lift out the moulds and invert them on a baking sheet. Transfer the ice creams to individual plates and sprinkle sliced pistachios over the top.

Coconut Ice

The creamy taste and texture of this ice cream comes from the natural fat content of coconut as the mixture contains neither cream nor egg and is very refreshing. The lime adds a delicious tangy flavour as well as pretty green specks to the finished ice. Decorate with toasted coconut shavings or toasted desiccated (dry unsweetened shredded) coconut (this browns very quickly, so watch it constantly).

SERVES FOUR TO SIX

115g/4oz/generous ½ cup caster (superfine) sugar

2 limes

400ml/14fl oz can coconut milk

toasted coconut shavings, to decorate (optional)

1 Pour 150ml/¼ pint/⅔ cup water in a small pan. Tip in the caster sugar and bring to the boil, stirring constantly until the sugar has completely dissolved. Remove the pan from the heat and leave the syrup to cool, then chill well.

2 Grate the rind from the limes finely, taking care to avoid the bitter pith. Squeeze out their juice and add to the pan of syrup with the rind. Add the coconut milk.

3 Pour the mixture into a freezerproof container and freeze for 5–6 hours, or until firm. Beat twice with a fork or electric whisk, or process in a food processor to break up the crystals. Scoop into dishes and decorate with toasted coconut shavings, if you like.

COOK'S TIP *To make toasted coconut shavings, rinse the flesh from a coconut under cold water. Shave slices using a vegetable peeler, then toast under a moderate grill (broiler) until they are curled and the edges have turned golden.*

Gingered Semi-freddo

This Italian ice cream is rather like the original soft scoop ice cream. Made with a boiled sugar syrup rather than a traditional egg custard, and generously speckled with chopped stem ginger, this delicious ice cream will stay soft when frozen. For a really impressive dinner party dessert, serve the semi-freddo in plain (semisweet) chocolate cases.

SERVES SIX

1 Mix the sugar and 120ml/4fl oz/½ cup cold water in a pan and heat gently, stirring occasionally, until the sugar has dissolved.

2 Increase the heat and boil for 4–5 minutes, without stirring, until the syrup registers 119°C/238°F on a sugar thermometer. Alternatively, test by dropping a little of the syrup into a cup of cold water. Pour the water away and you should be able to mould the syrup into a small ball.

3 Put the egg yolks in a large heatproof bowl and whisk until frothy. Place the bowl over a pan of simmering water and whisk in the sugar syrup. Continue whisking until the mixture is very thick. Remove from the heat and whisk until cool.

4 Whip the cream and lightly fold it into the egg yolk mixture with the chopped stem ginger. Pour into a freezerproof container and freeze for 1 hour.

5 Stir the semi-freddo to bring any ginger that has sunk to the base of the container to the top, then return it to the freezer for 5–6 hours, until firm. Scoop into dishes or chocolate cases (see Cook's Tip). Decorate with slices of ginger and serve.

115g/4oz/generous ½ cup caster (superfine) sugar

4 egg yolks

300ml/½ pint/1¼ cups double (heavy) cream

115g/4oz/⅔ cup drained stem (preserved) ginger, finely chopped, plus extra slices, to decorate

COOK'S TIP *To make the cases, pour melted chocolate over squares of baking parchment and drape them over upturned glasses. Peel off the baking parchment when set.*

Miniature Choc-ices

These little chocolate-coated ice creams make a fun alternative to the more familiar after-dinner chocolates, especially on hot summer evenings – although they need to be eaten quickly. Serve the choc-ices in fluted paper sweet (candy) cases. If you can, buy gold cases as they will contrast very prettily with the dark chocolate coating.

MAKES ABOUT TWENTY-FIVE

750ml/1¼ pints/ 3 cups vanilla, chocolate or coffee ice cream

200g/7oz plain (semisweet) chocolate, broken into pieces

25g/1oz milk chocolate, broken into pieces

25g/1oz/¼ cup chopped hazelnuts, lightly toasted

1 Put a large baking sheet in the freezer for 10 minutes. Using a melon baller, scoop balls of ice cream and place these on the baking sheet. Freeze for at least 1 hour or until firm.

2 Line a second baking sheet with baking parchment and place in the freezer for 15 minutes. Melt the plain chocolate in a heatproof bowl set over a pan of gently simmering water. Melt the milk chocolate in a separate bowl.

3 Using a metal spatula, transfer the ice cream scoops to the parchment-lined sheet. Spoon a little plain chocolate over one scoop so that most of it is coated.

4 Sprinkle immediately with chopped nuts, before the chocolate sets. Coat half the remaining scoops in the same way, sprinkling each one with nuts before the chocolate sets. Spoon the remaining plain chocolate over all the remaining scoops.

5 Using a teaspoon, drizzle the milk chocolate over the choc-ices that are not topped with nuts. Freeze again until ready to serve.

White Chocolate Castles

With a little ingenuity, good-quality bought ice cream can masquerade as a culinary masterpiece – it's down to perfect presentation. For a professional finish, dust the castles and plates with a hint of cocoa powder or icing (confectioners') sugar.

225g/8oz white chocolate, broken into pieces

250ml/8fl oz/1 cup white chocolate ice cream

250ml/8fl oz/1 cup dark chocolate ice cream

115g/4oz/1 cup berries

SERVES SIX

1 Put the white chocolate in a heatproof bowl, set it over a pan of gently simmering water and leave until melted. Line a baking sheet with greaseproof (waxed) paper. Cut out six 30 x 13cm/12 x 5in strips of greaseproof paper, then fold each in half lengthways.

2 Stand a 7.5cm/3in pastry (cookie) cutter on the baking sheet. Roll one strip of paper into a circle and fit inside the cutter with the folded edge on the base paper. Stick the edges together with tape.

3 Remove the cutter and shape more paper collars in the same way, leaving the pastry cutter in place around the final collar.

4 Spoon a little of the melted chocolate into the base of the collar supported by the cutter. Using a teaspoon, spread the chocolate over the base and up the sides of the collar, making the top edge uneven. Carefully lift away the cutter.

5 Make five more chocolate cases in the same way, using the cutter for extra support each time. Leave the cases in a cool place or in the refrigerator to set.

6 Carefully peel away the paper from the sides of the chocolate cases, then lift the cases off the base. Transfer to serving plates.

7 Using a large melon baller or teaspoon, scoop the white and dark chocolate ice creams into the cases and decorate with berries. Serve immediately.

Caramel and Pecan Terrine

Frozen or long-life cream is a useful ingredient for making impressive desserts without having a mega shopping trip. Caramel and nuts transform cream to parfait in this recipe. Take care that the syrup does not become too dark, or the ice cream will taste bitter.

SERVES SIX

115g/4oz/generous ½ cup sugar

450ml/¾ pint/scant 2 cups double (heavy) cream

30ml/2 tbsp icing (confectioners') sugar

75g/3oz/¾ cup pecan nuts, toasted

COOK'S TIP *Watch the caramel syrup closely after removing it from the heat. If it starts to turn too dark, dip the base of the pan in cold water. If the syrup remains very pale, return the pan to the heat and cook it for a little longer.*

1 Heat the sugar and 75ml/5 tbsp water in a small, heavy pan until the sugar dissolves. Boil rapidly until the sugar has turned pale golden. Remove the pan from the heat and leave to stand until the syrup turns a rich brown colour.

2 Pour 90ml/6 tbsp of the cream over the caramel. Heat to make a smooth sauce. Leave to cool.

3 Rinse a 450g/1lb loaf tin (pan), then line the base and sides with clear film (plastic wrap). Whip a further 150ml/¼ pint/⅔ cup of the cream with the icing sugar until it forms soft peaks. Whip the remaining cream separately and stir in the caramel sauce and the toasted pecan nuts.

4 Spoon one-third of the caramel cream into the prepared tin and spread with half the plain whipped cream. Spread half of the remaining caramel cream over the top, then top with the last of the plain cream. Finally, add the remaining caramel cream and level the surface. Freeze for 6 hours.

5 To serve, dip the tin in very hot water for 2 seconds, invert it on to a serving plate and peel away the film. Serve sliced.

White Chocolate and Brownie Torte

This delicious dessert is easy to make and guaranteed to appeal to just about everyone. If you can't buy good-quality brownies, use a moist chocolate sponge or make your own. For extra decoration, put a few fresh summer berries such as strawberries or raspberries around the edge or on the centre of the torte.

SERVES TEN

300g/11oz white chocolate, broken into pieces

600ml/1 pint/2½ cups double (heavy) cream

250g/9oz rich chocolate brownies

(unsweetened) cocoa powder, for dusting

1 Dampen the sides of a 20cm/8in springform tin (pan) and line with a strip of greaseproof (waxed) paper. Put the chocolate in a small pan. Add 150ml/¼ pint/⅔ cup of the cream and heat very gently until the chocolate has melted. Stir until smooth, then pour into a bowl and leave to cool.

2 Break the chocolate brownies into chunky pieces and sprinkle these over the base of the tin. Pack them down lightly to make a fairly dense base.

3 Whip the remaining cream until it forms peaks, then fold in the white chocolate mixture. Spoon into the tin to cover the layer of brownies, then tap the tin gently on the work surface to level the chocolate mixture. Cover and freeze overnight.

4 Transfer the torte to the refrigerator about 45 minutes before serving to soften slightly. Decorate with a light dusting of cocoa powder just before serving.

Soft Fruit and Meringue Gâteau

This recipe takes only five minutes to prepare but looks and tastes as though a lot of preparation went into it. The trick is to use really good vanilla ice cream. For a dinner party, slice the gâteau and place on individual plates, spoon ready-made strawberry or raspberry coulis around each slice and garnish with whole strawberries or raspberries.

SERVES SIX

1 Dampen a 900g/2lb loaf tin (pan) and line it with clear film (plastic wrap). If using strawberries, chop them into small pieces. Put them in a bowl and add the raspberries or redcurrants and icing sugar. Toss until the fruit is beginning to break up, but do not let it become mushy.

2 Put the ice cream in a bowl and break it up with a fork. Crumble the meringues into the bowl and add the soft fruit mixture.

3 Fold all the ingredients together until evenly combined and lightly marbled. Pack into the prepared tin and press down gently to level. Cover and freeze overnight. To serve, invert on to a plate and peel away the clear film. Serve in slices.

400g/14oz/3½ cups mixed small strawberries, raspberries and/ or redcurrants

30ml/2 tbsp icing (confectioners') sugar

750ml/1¼ pints/ 3 cups vanilla ice cream

6 meringue nests or 115g/4oz meringue

Cold Desserts

BECAUSE THEY CAN BE MADE IN ADVANCE, COLD DESSERTS

ARE THE PERFECT CHOICE FOR ENTERTAINING. ALL THE

RECIPES IN THIS CHAPTER HAVE AN ELEGANT SIMPLICITY

THAT GUARANTEES SUCCESS WITH EVEN THE MOST

SOPHISTICATED DINNER GUESTS. HOWEVER, THESE

DESSERTS ARE SO EASY TO PREPARE THAT YOU WILL WANT

TO SERVE THEM FOR EVERYDAY MEALS TOO.

Tropical Scented Fruit Salad

With its special colour and exotic flavour, this fresh fruit salad is perfect after a rich, heavy meal. For fabulous flavour and colour, try using three small blood oranges and three ordinary oranges. Other fruit that can be added include pears, kiwi fruit and bananas. Serve the fruit salad with whipping cream flavoured with 15g/½oz finely chopped drained preserved stem ginger.

SERVES FOUR TO SIX

1 Put the hulled and halved strawberries and peeled and segmented oranges into a serving bowl. Halve the passion fruit and using a teaspoon scoop the flesh into the bowl.

2 Pour the wine over the fruit and toss gently. Cover and chill in the refrigerator until ready to serve.

**350–400g/12–14oz/
3–3½ cups
strawberries, hulled
and halved**

**6 oranges, peeled
and segmented**

1–2 passion fruit

**120ml/4fl oz/½ cup
medium dry or
sweet white wine**

Juniper-scented Pears in Red Wine

More often used in savoury dishes than sweet, juniper berries have a dark blue, almost black colour with a distinct gin-like flavour. In this fruity winter dessert crushed juniper berries give the classic partnership of pears and red wine a slightly aromatic flavour. These pears are particularly good sprinkled with toasted almonds and whipped cream.

SERVES FOUR

1 Lightly crush the juniper berries using a pestle and mortar or with the end of a rolling pin. Put the berries in a pan with the sugar and wine and heat gently until the sugar dissolves.

2 Meanwhile, peel the pears, leaving them whole. Add them to the wine and heat until just simmering. Cover the pan and cook gently for about 25 minutes, until the pears are tender. Turn the pears once or twice to make sure they cook evenly.

3 Use a slotted spoon to remove the pears. Boil the syrup hard for a few minutes, until it is slightly reduced and thickened. If serving the pears hot, reheat them gently in the syrup, otherwise arrange them in a serving dish and spoon the syrup over.

30ml/2 tbsp juniper berries

50g/2oz/¼ cup caster (superfine) sugar

600ml/1 pint/2½ cups red wine

4 large or 8 small firm pears, stalks intact

Oranges in Syrup

This recipe works well with most citrus fruits – for example, try pink grapefruit or sweet, perfumed clementines, which have been peeled but left whole. Serve the oranges with 300ml/½ pint/1¼ cups whipped cream flavoured with 5ml/1 tsp ground cinnamon, or 5ml/1 tsp ground nutmeg or with Greek (US strained plain) yogurt.

SERVES SIX

6 medium oranges

200g/7oz/1 cup sugar

100ml/3½fl oz/ scant ½ cup fresh strong brewed coffee

50g/2oz/½ cup pistachio nuts, chopped (optional)

> **COOK'S TIP** *Choose a pan in which the oranges will just fit in a single layer – use a deep frying pan if you don't have a pan that is large enough.*

1 Finely pare, shred and reserve the rind from one orange. Peel the remaining oranges. Cut each one crossways into slices, then re-form them, with a cocktail stick (toothpick) through the centre.

2 Put the sugar in a heavy pan and add 50ml/2fl oz/¼ cup water. Heat gently until the sugar dissolves, then bring to the boil and cook until the syrup turns pale gold.

3 Remove from the heat and carefully pour 100ml/3½fl oz/ scant ½ cup freshly boiling water into the pan. Return to the heat until the syrup has dissolved in the water. Stir in the coffee.

4 Add the oranges and the rind to the coffee syrup. Simmer for 15–20 minutes, turning the oranges once during cooking. Leave to cool, then chill. Serve sprinkled with pistachio nuts, if using.

Fresh Fig Compote

A vanilla and coffee syrup brings out the wonderful flavour of figs – serve Greek (US strained plain) yogurt or vanilla ice cream with the poached fruit. A good selection of different honey is available – its aroma and flavour will be subtly scented by the plants surrounding the hives. Orange blossom honey works particularly well in this recipe, although any clear variety is suitable.

SERVES FOUR TO SIX

400ml/14fl oz/ 1⅔ cups fresh brewed coffee

115g/4oz/½ cup clear honey

1 vanilla pod (bean)

12 slightly under-ripe fresh figs

1 Choose a frying pan with a lid, large enough to hold the figs in a single layer. Pour in the coffee and add the honey.

2 Split the vanilla pod lengthways and scrape the seeds into the pan. Add the vanilla pod, then bring to a rapid boil and cook until reduced to about 175ml/6fl oz/¾ cup.

3 Wash the figs and pierce the skins several times with a sharp skewer. Cut in half and add to the syrup. Reduce the heat, cover and simmer for 5 minutes. Remove the figs from the syrup with a slotted spoon and set aside to cool.

4 Strain the syrup over the figs. Allow to stand at room temperature for 1 hour before serving.

> **COOK'S TIP** *Figs come in three main varieties – red, white and black – and all three are suitable for cooking. They are sweet and succulent, and complement the stronger, more pervasive flavours of coffee and vanilla very well.*

Baked Custard with Burnt Sugar

This delicious egg custard or crème brûlée is a rich indulgent dessert that can be prepared well in advance. You can buy vanilla sugar or make your own by placing a split vanilla pod (bean) in a jar of caster (superfine) sugar – the sugar will be ready to use after a couple of days.

SERVES SIX

1 Preheat the oven to 150°C/300°F/Gas 2. Place six 120ml/4fl oz/½ cup ramekins in a roasting pan or ovenproof dish and set aside while you prepare the vanilla custard.

2 Heat the double cream in a heavy pan over a gentle heat until it is very hot, but not boiling.

3 In a bowl, whisk the egg yolks and vanilla sugar until well blended. Whisk in the hot cream and strain into a large jug (pitcher). Divide the custard equally among the ramekins.

4 Pour enough boiling water into the roasting pan to come about halfway up the sides of the ramekins. Cover the pan with foil and bake for about 30 minutes, until the custards are just set. (Push the point of a knife into the centre of one; if it comes out clean, the custards are cooked.) Remove from the pan, cool, then chill.

5 Preheat the grill (broiler). Sprinkle the sugar evenly over the surface of the custards and grill (broil) for 30–60 seconds, until the sugar melts and caramelizes, taking care not to let it burn. Place in the refrigerator to chill and set the crust.

1 litre/1¾ pints/4 cups **double (heavy) cream**

6 egg yolks

90g/3½oz/½ cup **vanilla sugar**

75g/3oz/⅓ cup soft **light brown sugar**

COOK'S TIP *It is best to make the custards the day before you wish to eat them and chill overnight, so that they are really cold and firm.*

Passion Fruit Creams

These delicately perfumed creams are light with a fresh flavour from the passion fruit. Ripe passion fruit should look purple and wrinkled – choose fruit that are heavy for their size. When halved, the fragrant, sweet juicy flesh with small edible black seeds are revealed. These creams can be decorated with mint or geranium leaves and served with cream.

SERVES FIVE TO SIX

1 Preheat the oven to 180°C/350°F/Gas 4. Line the bases of six 120ml/4fl oz/½ cup ramekins with rounds of baking parchment and place them in a roasting pan.

2 Heat the cream to just below boiling point, then remove the pan from the heat. Sieve the flesh of four passion fruits and beat together with the sugar and eggs. Whisk in the hot cream and then ladle into the ramekins.

3 Half fill the roasting pan with boiling water. Bake the creams for 25–30 minutes, or until set, then leave to cool before chilling.

4 Run a knife around the insides of the ramekins, then invert them on to serving plates, tapping the bases firmly. Carefully peel off the baking parchment and chill in the refrigerator until ready to serve. Spoon on a little passion fruit flesh just before serving.

600ml/1 pint/2½ cups double (heavy) cream, or a mixture of single (light) and double (heavy) cream

6 passion fruits

30–45ml/2–3 tbsp vanilla sugar

5 eggs

Baked Caramel Custard

Many countries have their own version of this classic dessert. Known as *crème caramel* in France and *flan* in Spain, this chilled baked custard has a rich caramel flavour. By cooking the custard in a *bain-marie* or as here in a roasting pan with water, the mixture is cooked gently and the eggs are prevented from becoming tough or curdling. It is delicious served with fresh strawberries and thick cream.

SERVES SIX TO EIGHT

1 Put 175g/6oz/generous ¾ cup of the sugar in a small heavy pan with just enough water to moisten the sugar. Bring to the boil over a high heat, swirling the pan until the sugar has dissolved completely. Boil for about 5 minutes, without stirring, until the syrup turns a rich, dark caramel colour.

2 Working quickly, pour the caramel into a 1 litre/ 1¾ pint/4 cup soufflé dish. Holding the dish with oven gloves, carefully swirl it to coat the base and sides with the hot caramel mixture. Set aside to cool.

3 Preheat the oven to 160°C/325°F/Gas 3. In a bowl, whisk the eggs and egg yolks with the remaining sugar for 2–3 minutes, until smooth and creamy.

4 Heat the cream in a heavy pan until hot, but not boiling. Whisk the hot cream into the egg mixture and carefully strain the mixture into the caramel-lined dish. Cover tightly with foil.

5 Place the dish in a roasting pan and pour in just enough boiling water to come halfway up the side of the dish. Bake the custard for 40–45 minutes, until just set. To test whether the custard is set, insert a knife about 5cm/2in from the edge; if the blade comes out clean, the custard should be ready.

6 Remove the soufflé dish from the roasting pan and leave to cool for at least 30 minutes, then place in the refrigerator and chill overnight.

7 To turn out, carefully run a sharp knife around the edge of the dish to loosen the custard. Cover the dish with a serving plate and, holding them both together very tightly, invert the dish and plate, allowing the custard to drop down on to the plate.

8 Gently lift one edge of the dish, allowing the caramel to run down over the sides and on to the plate, then carefully lift off the dish. Serve immediately.

250g/9oz/1¼ cups vanilla sugar

5 large (US extra large) eggs, plus 2 extra yolks

450ml/¾ pint/scant 2 cups double (heavy) cream

VARIATION

For a special occasion, make individual baked custards in ramekin dishes. Coat six to eight ramekins with the caramel and divide the custard mixture among them. Bake, in a roasting pan of water, for 25–30 minutes or until set. Thinly slice the strawberries and marinate them in a little sugar and a liqueur or dessert wine, such as Amaretto or Muscat wine.

Chilled Chocolate and Espresso Mousse

Heady, aromatic espresso coffee adds a distinctive flavour to this smooth, rich mousse. For a special occasion, serve the mousse in stylish chocolate cups decorated with sprigs of mint, with mascarpone or clotted cream on the side.

SERVES FOUR

450g/1lb plain (semisweet) chocolate

45ml/3 tbsp freshly brewed espresso

25g/1oz/2 tbsp unsalted (sweet) butter

4 eggs, separated

1 For each chocolate cup, cut a double thickness 15cm/6in square of foil. Mould it around a small orange, leaving the edges and corners loose to make a cup shape. Remove the orange and press the bottom of the foil case gently on a surface to make a flat base. Repeat to make four foil cups.

2 Break half the chocolate into small pieces and place in a bowl set over a pan of very hot water. Stir occasionally until the chocolate has completely melted.

3 Spoon the chocolate into the foil cups, spreading it up the sides with the back of a spoon to give a ragged edge. Chill for 30 minutes in the refrigerator, or until set hard. Gently peel away the foil, starting at the top edge.

4 To make the chocolate mousse, put the remaining chocolate and espresso into a bowl set over a pan of hot water and melt as before, until smooth and liquid. Stir in the butter, a little at a time. Remove the pan from the heat and then stir in the egg yolks.

5 Whisk the egg whites in a bowl until stiff, but not dry, then fold them into the chocolate mixture. Pour into a bowl and chill for at least 3 hours, or until the mousse is set. Scoop the chilled mousse into the chocolate cups just before serving.

Meringue Pyramid with Chocolate Mascarpone

This impressive cake makes a perfect centrepiece for a celebration buffet. Dust the pyramid with a little sieved icing (confectioners') sugar and sprinkle with just a few rose petals for simple but stunning presentation.

SERVES ABOUT TEN

200g/7oz plain (semisweet) chocolate

4 egg whites

150g/5oz/¾ cup caster (superfine) sugar

115g/4oz/½ cup mascarpone cheese

1 Preheat the oven to 150°C/300°F/Gas 2. Line two large baking sheets with baking parchment or greaseproof (waxed) paper. Grate 75g/3oz of the chocolate.

2 Whisk the egg whites in a clean, grease-free bowl until they form stiff peaks. Gradually whisk in half the sugar, then add the rest and whisk until the meringue is very stiff and glossy. Add the grated chocolate and whisk lightly to mix.

3 Draw a 20cm/8in circle on the lining paper on one of the baking sheets, turn it upside down, and spread the marked circle evenly with about half the meringue. Spoon the remaining meringue in 28–30 teaspoonfuls on both baking sheets. Bake the meringue for 1–1½ hours, or until crisp and completely dried out.

4 Make the filling. Melt the remaining chocolate in a heatproof bowl over hot water. Cool slightly, then stir in the mascarpone. Cool the mixture until firm.

5 Spoon the chocolate mixture into a large piping (pastry) bag and use to sandwich the meringues together in pairs, reserving a small amount of filling for the pyramid.

6 Arrange the filled meringues on a serving platter, piling them up in a pyramid and keeping them in position with a few well-placed dabs of the reserved filling.

COOK'S TIP

The meringues can be made up to a week in advance and stored in a cool, dry place in an airtight container.

Classic Chocolate Roulade

This rich, squidgy chocolate roll should be made at least eight hours before serving to allow it to soften. Expect the roulade to crack a little when you roll it up – sprinkle with a little grated chocolate, if you like, as a final decoration. When melting chocolate, break it into even-sized pieces and place in a dry heatproof bowl over hot water. If the water is too hot the chocolate will turn grainy and scorch; if the chocolate is splashed with water it will harden and acquire a dull finish.

SERVES EIGHT

1 Preheat the oven to 180°C/350°F/Gas 4. Grease and line a 33 x 23cm/13 x 9in Swiss (jelly) roll tin (pan) with baking parchment.

2 Break the chocolate into squares and melt in a bowl over a pan of barely simmering water. Remove from the heat and leave to cool for about 5 minutes.

3 In a large bowl, whisk the sugar and egg yolks until light and fluffy. Stir in the melted chocolate.

4 Whisk the egg whites until stiff, but not dry, and then gently fold into the chocolate mixture.

5 Pour the chocolate mixture into the prepared tin, spreading it level with a palette knife (metal spatula). Bake for about 25 minutes, or until firm. Leave the cake in the tin and cover with a cooling rack, making sure that it does not touch the cake.

6 Cover the rack with a damp dishtowel, then wrap in clear film (plastic wrap). Leave in a cool place for 8 hours, preferably overnight.

7 Dust a sheet of greaseproof (waxed) paper with caster or icing sugar and turn out the roulade on to it. Peel off the lining paper.

8 To make the filling, whip the double cream until soft peaks form. Spread the cream over the roulade. Starting from one of the short ends, carefully roll it up, using the paper to help.

9 Place the roulade, seam side down, on to a serving plate and dust generously with more caster or icing sugar before serving.

200g/7oz plain (semisweet) chocolate

200g/7oz/1 cup caster (superfine) sugar, plus extra caster or icing (confectioners') sugar to dust

7 eggs, separated

300ml/½ pint/1¼ cups double (heavy) cream

COOK'S TIP

For a special dessert, decorate the roulade with swirls of whipped cream and chocolate coffee beans or with clusters of raspberries and mint leaves.

Summer Fruit Brioche

Scooped-out, individual brioches make perfect containers for the fruity filling in this stylish, but simple dessert. If small brioches are not available, serve the fruit on slices cut from a large brioche. Any summer fruits can be used in this dessert – try raspberries, sliced peaches, nectarines, apricots, or pitted cherries. Serve with single (light) cream poured over.

SERVES FOUR

1 Preheat the grill (broiler). Slice the tops off the brioches and use a teaspoon to scoop out their centres, leaving a 1 cm/½in thick case. Lightly toast them, turning once and watching them carefully, as they will brown very quickly.

2 Put the strawberries in a pan with the sugar and add 60ml/4 tbsp water. Heat very gently for about 1 minute, until the strawberries are softened but still keep their shape. Remove the pan from the heat, stir in the raspberries and leave to cool.

3 Place the brioches on plates and pile the fruit mixture into them. Add plenty of juice to saturate the brioches and allow it to flood the plates. Place any extra fruit on the plates.

4 individual brioches

300g/11oz/ 2½ cups small ripe strawberries, halved

30ml/2 tbsp caster (superfine) sugar

115g/4oz/⅔ cup raspberries

Rhubarb and Ginger Jellies

Made with bright pink, young rhubarb, these softly set jellies get the taste buds tingling. They are spiced with plenty of fresh ginger, which gives just a hint of zesty warmth. Pour the jelly into pretty glasses and serve it as it is or top it with spoonfuls of lightly whipped cream.

SERVES FIVE TO SIX

1kg/2¼lb young rhubarb

200g/7oz/1 cup caster (superfine) sugar

50g/2oz fresh root ginger, finely chopped

15ml/1 tbsp powdered gelatine

1 Cut the rhubarb into 2cm/¾in chunks and place in a pan with the sugar and ginger. Pour in 450ml/¾ pint/scant 2 cups water and bring to the boil. Reduce the heat, cover and simmer gently for 10 minutes, until the rhubarb is very soft and pulpy.

2 Meanwhile, sprinkle the gelatine over 30ml/2 tbsp cold water in a small heatproof bowl. Leave to stand, without stirring, for 5 minutes, until the gelatine has become sponge-like in texture. Set the bowl over a small pan of hot water and simmer, stirring occasionally, until the gelatine has dissolved completely into a clear liquid. Remove from the heat.

3 Strain the cooked rhubarb through a fine sieve into a bowl. Stir in the dissolved gelatine until thoroughly mixed. Leave to cool slightly before pouring into serving glasses. Chill for at least 4 hours or overnight, until set.

Hot Desserts

A HOT DESSERT MAKES THE PERFECT END TO A MEAL
AND CAN TAKE VERY LITTLE TIME TO PREPARE. A FEW
WELL-CHOSEN INGREDIENTS CAN BE TURNED INTO A
SUMPTUOUS, MOUTHWATERING TREAT WITH THE MINIMUM
OF EFFORT. MANY OF THE RECIPES IN THIS CHAPTER CAN
BE PREPARED IN ADVANCE AND SIMPLY POPPED IN THE
OVEN TO COOK WHILE YOU SERVE THE MAIN COURSE.

Grilled Peaches with Meringues

Ripe peaches take on a fabulous scented fruitiness when grilled with brown sugar, and mini meringues are the perfect accompaniment. Serve with crème fraîche flavoured with a little grated orange rind. When buying peaches or nectarines, choose fruit with an attractive rosy bloom, avoiding any that have a green-tinged skin or feel hard. Nectarines have a smoother skin than peaches and are actually a type of peach native to China.

2 egg whites

115g/4oz/½ cup soft light brown sugar, reserving 5ml/1 tsp for the peaches

pinch of ground cinnamon

6 ripe peaches, or nectarines

SERVES SIX

1 Preheat the oven to 140°C/275°F/Gas 1. Line two large baking sheets with baking parchment.

2 Whisk the egg whites until they form stiff peaks. Gradually whisk in the sugar and ground cinnamon until the mixture is stiff and glossy. Pipe 18 very small meringues on to the trays and bake for 40 minutes. Leave in the oven to cool.

3 Meanwhile, halve and stone (pit) the peaches or nectarines, sprinkling each half with a little sugar as it is cut. Grill (broil) for 4–5 minutes, until just beginning to caramelize.

4 Arrange the grilled peaches on serving plates with the meringues and serve immediately.

COOK'S TIP

Use leftover egg whites to make these little cinnamon-flavoured meringues. The meringues can be stored in an airtight container for about 2 weeks. Serve them after dinner with coffee or with desserts in place of biscuits (cookies).

Summer Berries in Sabayon Glaze

This luxurious combination of summer berries under a light and fluffy liqueur sauce is lightly grilled to form a crisp, caramelized topping. Fresh or frozen berries can be used in this dessert. If you use frozen berries, defrost them in a sieve over a bowl to allow the juices to drip. Stir a little juice into the fruit before dividing among the dishes.

SERVES FOUR

1 Arrange the mixed summer berries or soft fruit in four individual flameproof dishes. Preheat the grill (broiler).

2 Whisk the yolks in a large bowl with the sugar and liqueur or wine. Place over a pan of hot water and whisk constantly until the mixture is thick, fluffy and pale.

3 Pour equal quantities of the yolk mixture into each dish. Place under the grill for 1–2 minutes, until just turning brown. Add an extra splash of liqueur, if you like, and serve immediately.

450g/1lb/4 cups mixed summer berries, or soft fruit

4 egg yolks

50g/2oz/¼ cup vanilla sugar or caster (superfine) sugar

120ml/4fl oz/½ cup liqueur, such as Cointreau or Kirsch, or a white dessert wine

Zabaglione

Light as air and wonderfully heady, this warm, wine egg custard is a much-loved Italian dessert. Traditionally made with Sicilian Marsala, other fortified wines such as Madeira or sweet sherry can be used.

SERVES FOUR

1 Place the egg yolks and sugar in a large heatproof bowl and whisk with an electric beater until the mixture is pale and thick.

2 Gradually add the Marsala, Madeira or sweet sherry to the egg mixture, 15ml/1 tbsp at a time, whisking well after each addition.

3 Place the bowl over a pan of gently simmering water and whisk for 5–7 minutes, until thick: when the beaters are lifted, they should leave a thick trail on the surface of the mixture. Do not be tempted to give up when beating the mixture, as the zabaglione will be too runny and will be likely to separate if it is underbeaten.

4 Pour into four warmed, stemmed glasses and serve immediately, with amaretti for dipping.

4 egg yolks

50g/2oz/¼ cup caster (superfine) sugar

60ml/4 tbsp Marsala, Madeira or sweet sherry

amaretti biscuits, to serve

EXTRAS *Marinate chopped strawberries in a little extra Marsala, Madeira or sweet sherry for an hour or so. Sweeten with sugar, if you like, and spoon into glasses before you add the zabaglione.*

Apricot and Ginger Gratin

Made with tangy fresh apricots, this quick and easy dessert has a comforting, baked cheesecake-like flavour. For an even easier version of this delicious gratin, use 400g/14oz canned apricots in juice. Use juice from the can to beat into the cream cheese.

SERVES FOUR

1 Put the apricots in a pan with the sugar. Pour in 75ml/5 tbsp water and heat until barely simmering. Cover and cook very gently for 8–10 minutes, until they are tender but still holding their shape.

2 Preheat the oven to 200°C/400°F/Gas 6. Drain the apricots, reserving the syrup, and place in a large dish or divide among four individual ovenproof dishes. Set aside 90ml/6 tbsp of the syrup and spoon the remainder over the fruit.

3 Beat the cream cheese until softened, then gradually beat in the reserved syrup until smooth. Spoon the cheese mixture over the apricots. Sprinkle the biscuit crumbs over the cream cheese and juice mixture. Bake for 10 minutes, until the crumb topping is beginning to darken and the filling has warmed through. Serve immediately.

500g/1¼ lb apricots, halved and stoned (pitted)

75g/3oz/scant ½ cup caster (superfine) sugar

200g/7oz/scant 1 cup cream cheese

75g/3oz gingernut biscuits (gingersnaps), crushed to crumbs

Baked Ricotta Cakes with Red Sauce

These honey-flavoured desserts take only minutes to make from a few ingredients. The fragrant fruity sauce provides a contrast of both colour and flavour. The red berry sauce can be made a day in advance and chilled until ready to use. Frozen fruit doesn't need extra water, as it usually yields its juice easily on thawing.

SERVES FOUR

250g/9oz/generous 1 cup ricotta cheese

2 egg whites, beaten

60ml/4 tbsp scented honey, plus extra to taste

450g/1lb/4 cups mixed fresh or frozen fruit, such as strawberries, raspberries, blackberries and cherries

1 Preheat the oven to 180°C/350°F/Gas 4. Place the ricotta cheese in a bowl and break it up with a wooden spoon. Add the beaten egg whites and honey, and mix thoroughly until smooth and well combined.

2 Lightly grease four ramekins. Spoon the ricotta mixture into the prepared ramekins and level the tops. Bake for 20 minutes, or until the ricotta cakes are risen and golden.

3 Meanwhile, make the fruit sauce. Reserve about one-quarter of the fruit for decoration. Place the rest of the fruit in a pan, with a little water if the fruit is fresh, and heat gently until softened. Leave to cool slightly and remove any stones (pits) if using cherries.

4 Press the fruit through a sieve, then taste and sweeten with honey if it is too tart. Serve the sauce, warm or cold, with the ricotta cakes. Decorate with the reserved berries.

Hot Blackberry and Apple Soufflé

The deliciously tart flavours of blackberry and apple complement each other perfectly to make a light, mouthwatering and surprisingly low-fat, hot dessert. Running a table knife around the inside edge of the soufflé dishes before baking helps the soufflés to rise evenly without sticking to the rim of the dish. Make this dish in early autumn, when there are plentiful supplies of blackberries.

MAKES SIX

1 Preheat the oven to 200°C/400°F/Gas 6. Put a baking sheet in the oven to heat. Cook the blackberries and apple in a pan for 10 minutes, or until the juice runs from the blackberries and the apple has pulped down well. Press through a sieve into a bowl. Stir in 50g/2oz/¼ cup caster sugar. Set aside to cool.

2 Put a spoonful of the fruit purée into each of six 150ml/¼ pint/⅔ cup greased and sugared individual soufflé dishes and smooth the surface. Set the dishes aside.

3 Whisk the egg whites in a large bowl until they form stiff peaks. Gradually whisk in the remaining caster sugar. Fold in the remaining fruit purée and spoon the flavoured meringue into the prepared dishes. Level the tops with a palette knife (metal spatula) and run a table knife around the edge of each dish.

4 Place the dishes on the hot baking sheet and bake for 10–15 minutes, until the soufflés have risen well and are lightly browned. Dust the tops with a little sugar and serve immediately.

350g/12oz/3 cups blackberries

1 large cooking apple, peeled and finely diced

3 egg whites

150g/5oz/¾ cup caster (superfine) sugar, plus extra caster or icing (confectioners') sugar for dusting

Warm Chocolate Zabaglione

Once you've tasted this sensuous dessert, you'll never regard cocoa in quite the same way again. The zabaglione can be dusted with icing (confectioners') sugar instead of extra cocoa, if you like. Serve with mini amaretti or other small, crisp biscuits (cookies).

SERVES SIX

6 egg yolks

150g/5oz/¾ cup caster (superfine) sugar

45ml/3 tbsp (unsweetened) cocoa powder, plus extra for dusting

200ml/7fl oz/scant 1 cup Marsala

1 Prepare a pan of simmering water and a heatproof bowl to fit on top. Place the egg yolks and sugar in the bowl and whisk, off the heat, until the mixture is pale and all the sugar has dissolved.

2 Add the cocoa and Marsala, then place the bowl over the simmering water. Beat with a hand-held electric mixer until the mixture is smooth, thick and foamy.

3 Pour quickly into tall glasses, dust lightly with cocoa and serve immediately, with amaretti or other dessert biscuits, if liked.

Hot Chocolate Rum Soufflés

Light as air, melt-in-the-mouth soufflés are always impressive, yet they are often based on the simplest store-cupboard ingredients. Serve them as soon as they are cooked for a fantastic finale to a special dinner party. For an extra indulgent touch, serve the soufflés with whipped cream flavoured with dark rum and grated orange rind.

SERVES SIX

50g/2oz/½ cup (unsweetened) cocoa powder

65g/2½oz/5 tbsp caster (superfine) sugar, plus extra caster or icing (confectioners') sugar for dusting

30ml/2 tbsp dark rum

6 egg whites

1 Preheat the oven to 190°C/375°F/Gas 3. Place a baking sheet in the oven to heat up.

2 Mix 15ml/1 tbsp of the cocoa with 15ml/1 tbsp of the sugar in a bowl. Grease six 250ml/8fl oz/1 cup ramekins. Pour the cocoa and sugar mixture into each of the dishes in turn, rotating them so that they are evenly coated.

3 Mix the remaining cocoa powder with the dark rum.

4 Whisk the egg whites in a clean, grease-free bowl until they form stiff peaks. Whisk in the remaining sugar. Stir a generous spoonful of the whites into the cocoa mixture to lighten it, then fold in the remaining whites.

5 Divide the mixture among the dishes. Place on the hot baking sheet, and bake for 13–15 minutes, or until well risen. Dust with caster or icing sugar before serving.

COOK'S TIP *When serving the soufflés at the end of a dinner party, prepare them just before the meal is served. Put them in the oven when the main course is finished and serve steaming hot.*

Caramelized Upside-down Pear Pie

In this gloriously sticky dessert, which is almost like the French classic *tarte tatin*, the pastry is baked on top of the fruit, which gives it a crisp and flaky texture. When inverted, the pie looks wonderful. Look for good-quality chilled pastry that you can freeze for future use. Serve with whipped cream, ice cream or just plain for a gloriously sticky dessert.

SERVES EIGHT

1 Peel, quarter and core the pears. Toss with some of the sugar in a bowl.

2 Melt the butter in a 27cm/10½in heavy, ovenproof omelette pan. Add the remaining sugar. When it changes colour, arrange the pears in the pan.

3 Continue cooking, uncovered, for 20 minutes, or until the fruit has completely caramelized.

4 Leave the fruit to cool in the pan. Preheat the oven to 200°C/400°F/Gas 6. Meanwhile, on a lightly floured surface, roll out the pastry to a round that is slightly larger than the diameter of the pan. Lay the pastry on top of the pears and then carefully tuck it in around the edge.

5 Bake for 15 minutes, then lower the oven temperature to 180°C/350°F/Gas 4. Bake for a further 15 minutes, or until the pastry is golden.

6 Let the pie cool in the pan for a few minutes. To unmould, run a knife around the pan's edge, then, using oven gloves, invert a plate over the pan and quickly turn the two over together.

7 If any pears stick to the pan, remove them gently with a palette knife (metal spatula) and replace them on the pie. The pie is best served warm.

5–6 firm, ripe pears

175g/6oz/scant 1 cup caster (superfine) sugar

115g/4oz/½ cup butter

225g/8oz (unsweetened) shortcrust pastry

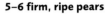

VARIATIONS

• To make caramelized upside-down apple pie, replace the pears with eight or nine firm, full-flavoured eating apples – Cox's Orange Pippins would be a good choice. You will need more apples than pears, as they shrink during cooking.

• Nectarines or peaches also work well, as does rhubarb. Rhubarb is tart, so you may need to add more sugar.

Peach Pie

Fruit pies do not have to be restricted to the chunky, deep-dish variety. Here, juicy, ripe peaches are encased in crisp pastry to make a glorious puffed dome – simple but delicious. For a really crispy crust, glaze the pie with beaten egg yolk thinned with a little water before sprinkling with sugar. Serve the pie with good quality vanilla ice cream or clotted cream.

SERVES EIGHT

1 Blanch the peaches for 30 seconds. Drain, refresh in cold water, then peel. Halve, stone (pit) and slice the peaches.

2 Melt the butter in a large frying pan. Add the peach slices, then sprinkle with 15ml/1 tbsp water and the sugar. Cook for about 4 minutes, shaking the pan frequently, or until the sugar has dissolved and the peaches are tender. Set the pan aside to cool.

3 Cut the pastry into two pieces, one slightly larger than the other. Roll out on a lightly floured surface and, using plates as a guide, cut a 30cm/12in round and a 28cm/11in round. Place the pastry rounds on baking sheets lined with baking parchment, cover with clear film (plastic wrap) and chill for 30 minutes.

4 Preheat the oven to 200°C/400°F/Gas 6. Remove the clear film from the pastry rounds. Spoon the peaches into the middle of the larger round and spread them out to within 5cm/2in of the edge. Place the smaller pastry round on top. Brush the edge of the larger pastry round with water, then fold this over the top round and press to seal. Twist the edges together.

5 Lightly brush the pastry with water and sprinkle evenly with a little sugar. Make five or six small crescent-shape slashes on the top of the pastry. Bake the pie for about 45 minutes and serve warm.

6 large, firm ripe peaches

40g/1½oz/ 3 tbsp butter

75g/3oz/6 tbsp caster (superfine) sugar, plus extra for glazing

450g/1lb puff pastry

EXTRAS
Brandy, peach liqueur or peach schnapps would be superb with the peaches in this pie: add 45ml/3 tbsp instead of the water in step 2.

Treacle Tart

The best chilled commercial shortcrust pastry makes light work of this old-fashioned favourite, with its sticky filling and twisted lattice topping. Smooth creamy custard is the classic accompaniment, but it is also delicious served with cream or ice cream. For a more textured filling, use wholemeal (whole-wheat) breadcrumbs or crushed cornflakes instead of the white breadcrumbs.

SERVES FOUR TO SIX

1 On a lightly floured surface, roll out three-quarters of the pastry to a thickness of 3mm/⅛in. Transfer to a 20cm/8in fluted flan tin (quiche pan) and trim off the overhang. Chill the pastry case (pie shell) for 20 minutes. Reserve the pastry trimmings.

2 Put a baking sheet in the oven and preheat to 200°C/400°F/ Gas 6. To make the filling, warm the syrup in a pan until it melts. Grate the lemon rind and squeeze the juice.

3 Remove the syrup from the heat and stir in the breadcrumbs and lemon rind. Leave to stand for 10 minutes, then add more crumbs if the mixture is too thin and moist. Stir in 30ml/2 tbsp of the lemon juice, then spread the mixture evenly in the pastry case.

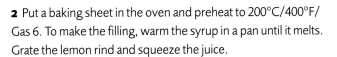

4 Roll out the reserved pastry and cut into 10–12 thin strips. Twist the strips into spirals, then lay half of them on the filling. Arrange the remaining strips at right angles to form a lattice. Press the ends on to the rim.

5 Place the tart on the hot baking sheet and bake for 10 minutes. Lower the oven temperature to 190°C/375°F/Gas 5. Bake for 15 minutes more, until golden. Serve warm.

350g/12oz (unsweetened) shortcrust pastry

260g/9½oz/generous ¾ cup golden (light corn) syrup

1 lemon

75g/3oz/1½ cups fresh white breadcrumbs

Blueberry and Almond Tart

This is a cheat's version of a sweet almond tart and the result is superb. Whisked egg whites and grated marzipan cook to form a light sponge under a tangy topping of contrasting blueberries. When whisking the egg whites for the filling, ensure all traces of yolk are removed – otherwise you won't be able to whisk them to their maximum volume.

SERVES SIX

**250g/9oz
(unsweetened)
shortcrust pastry**

**175g/6oz/generous
1 cup white marzipan**

**4 large (US extra large)
egg whites**

**130g/4½oz/
generous 1 cup
blueberries**

1 Preheat the oven to 200°C/400°F/Gas 6. Roll out the pastry and use to line a 23cm/9in round, loose-based flan tin (quiche pan). Line with greaseproof (waxed) paper and fill with baking beans, then bake for 15 minutes. Remove the beans and greaseproof paper and bake for a further 5 minutes. Reduce the oven temperature to 180°C/350°F/Gas 4.

2 Grate the marzipan. Whisk the egg whites until stiff. Sprinkle half the marzipan over them and fold in. Then fold in the rest.

3 Turn the mixture into the pastry case (pie shell) and spread it evenly. Sprinkle the blueberries over the top and bake for 20–25 minutes, until golden and just set. Leave to cool for 10 minutes before serving.

Baked Bananas with Ice Cream and Toffee Sauce

Bananas make one of the easiest of all desserts, just as welcome as a comforting winter treat as they are to follow a barbecue. For an extra sweet finishing touch, grate some plain (semisweet) chocolate on the bananas, over the sauce, just before serving. If baking on a barbecue, turn the bananas occasionally to ensure even cooking.

SERVES FOUR

4 large bananas

75g/3oz/scant ½ cup light muscovado (brown) sugar

75ml/5 tbsp double (heavy) cream

4 scoops good-quality vanilla ice cream

1 Preheat the oven to 180°C/350°F/Gas 4. Put the unpeeled bananas in an ovenproof dish and bake for 15–20 minutes, until the skins are very dark and the flesh feels soft when squeezed.

2 Meanwhile, heat the light muscovado sugar in a small, heavy pan with 75ml/5 tbsp water until dissolved. Bring to the boil and add the double cream. Cook for 5 minutes, until the sauce has thickened and is toffee coloured. Remove from the heat.

3 Transfer the baked bananas in their skins to serving plates and split them lengthways to reveal the flesh. Pour some of the sauce over the bananas and top with scoops of vanilla ice cream. Serve any remaining sauce separately.

Cakes, Cookies and Sweetmeats

HOME-BAKED CAKES AND SWEET SNACKS ARE THE
ULTIMATE INDULGENCE BUT ARE VIEWED BY MANY AS
TAKING TOO MUCH TIME AND EFFORT. HOWEVER, WITH
JUST A FEW BASIC INGREDIENTS, YOU CAN WHIP UP
FABULOUS CAKES, COOKIES AND CANDIES IN MOMENTS.
TRY DELICIOUS TREATS SUCH AS CHOCOLATE BROWNIES,
CHEWY FLAPJACKS OR QUICK AND EASY TEABREAD.

Chewy Flapjacks

Flapjacks are popular with adults and children alike and they are so quick and easy to make. For alternative versions of the basic recipe, stir in 50g/2oz/¼ cup finely chopped ready-to-eat dried apricots or sultanas (golden raisins). To make a really decadent treat, you can dip the cooled flapjack fingers into melted chocolate, to half cover.

MAKES TWELVE

1 Preheat the oven to 180°C/350°F/Gas 4. Line the base and sides of a 20cm/8in square cake tin (pan) with baking parchment.

2 Mix the butter, sugar and syrup in a pan and heat gently until the butter has melted. Add the oats and stir until all the ingredients are combined. Turn the mixture into the tin and level the surface.

3 Bake the flapjacks for 15–20 minutes, until just beginning to turn golden. Leave to cool slightly, then cut into fingers and remove from the tin. Store in an airtight container.

175g/6oz/¾ cup unsalted (sweet) butter

50g/2oz/¼ cup caster (superfine) sugar

150g/5oz/generous ⅓ cup golden (light corn) syrup

250g/9oz/2¾ cups rolled oats

Quick and Easy Teabread

This succulent, fruity teabread can be served just as it is, or spread with a little butter. The loaf can be stored, tightly wrapped in foil or in an airtight container, for up to five days. A great way to get children to eat some fruit, this teabread is ideal for packed lunches, picnics, or simply served with a cup of tea for afternoon tea.

SERVES EIGHT

1 Put the fruit in a bowl. Add 150ml/¼ pint/⅔ cup boiling water and leave to stand for 30 minutes.

2 Preheat the oven to 180°C/350°F/Gas 4. Grease and line the base and long sides of a 450g/1lb loaf tin (pan).

3 Beat the main quantity of sugar and the egg into the fruit. Sift the flour into the bowl and stir until combined. Turn into the prepared tin and level the surface. Sprinkle with the remaining sugar.

4 Bake the teabread for about 50 minutes, until risen and firm to the touch. When the bread is cooked, a skewer inserted into the centre will come out without any sticky mixture on it. Leave the loaf in the tin for 10 minutes before turning out on to a wire rack to cool.

350g/12oz/2 cups luxury mixed dried fruit

75g/3oz/scant ⅓ cup demerara (raw) sugar, plus 15ml/1 tbsp

1 large (US extra large) egg

175g/6oz/1½ cups self-raising (self-rising) flour

Orange and Pecan Scones

Serve these nutty orange scones with satiny orange or lemon curd or, for a simple, unsweetened snack, fresh and warm with unsalted (sweet) butter. Scones are best served on the day they are made, or they can be frozen. To freeze, place in an airtight container. To thaw, remove from the freezer and thaw at room temperature for an hour.

MAKES TEN

1 Preheat the oven to 220°C/425°F/Gas 7. Grease a baking sheet. Put the flour in a food processor with a pinch of salt and add the butter. Process the mixture until it resembles coarse breadcrumbs.

2 Add the orange rind. Reserve 30ml/2 tbsp of the orange juice and make the remainder up to 120ml/4fl oz/½ cup with water. Add the nuts and the juice mixture to the processor, process very briefly to a firm dough, adding a little water if the dough feels dry.

3 Turn the dough out on to a lightly floured surface and roll out to 2cm/¾ in thick. Cut out scones using a round cutter and transfer them to the baking sheet. Re-roll the trimmings and cut more scones. Brush the scones with the reserved juice and bake for 15–20 minutes, until golden. Transfer to a wire rack to cool.

225g/8oz/2 cups self-raising (self-rising) flour

50g/2oz/¼ cup unsalted (sweet) butter, chilled and diced

grated rind and juice of 1 orange

115g/4oz/1 cup pecan nuts, coarsely chopped

Creamed Coconut Macaroons

Finely grated creamed coconut gives these soft-centred cookies a rich creaminess. Cooking the gooey mixture on baking parchment makes sure that the cookies are easily removed from the baking sheet. For a tangy flavour, add the grated rind of one lime to the mixture in step 2. The cooked macaroons can be stored in an airtight container for up to one week.

MAKES SIXTEEN TO EIGHTEEN

1 Preheat the oven to 180°C/350°F/Gas 4. Line a large baking sheet with baking parchment. Finely grate the creamed coconut.

2 Use an electric beater to whisk the egg whites in a large bowl until stiff. Whisk in the sugar, a little at a time, to make a stiff and glossy meringue. Fold in the grated creamed and desiccated coconut, using a large, metal spoon.

3 Place dessertspoonfuls of the mixture, spaced slightly apart, on the baking sheet. Bake for 15–20 minutes, until slightly risen and golden brown. Leave to cool on the parchment, then transfer to an airtight container.

50g/2oz creamed coconut, chilled

2 large (US extra large) egg whites

90g/3½oz/ ½ cup caster (superfine) sugar

75g/3oz/1 cup desiccated (dry unsweetened shredded) coconut

Rich Chocolate Brownies

These brownies are packed with both milk and plain chocolate instead of adding sugar to the mixture. Serve them in small squares as they are very rich. When buying plain chocolate, bear in mind that the higher the percentage of cocoa solids, the higher the quality of the chocolate, and the less sugar it contains. The best quality has 70 per cent cocoa solids.

MAKES SIXTEEN

1 Preheat the oven to 180°C/350°F/Gas 4. Line the base and sides of a 20cm/8in square cake tin (pan) with baking parchment.

2 Break the plain chocolate and 90g/3½oz of the milk chocolate into pieces and put in a heatproof bowl with the butter. Melt over a pan of barely simmering water, stirring frequently.

3 Chop the remaining milk chocolate into chunky pieces. Stir the flour and eggs into the melted chocolate until evenly combined. Stir in half the chopped milk chocolate and turn the mixture into the prepared tin, spreading it into the corners. Sprinkle with the remaining chopped chocolate.

4 Bake the brownies for 30–35 minutes, until risen and just firm to the touch. Leave to cool in the tin, then cut the mixture into squares. Store the brownies in an airtight container.

300g/11oz each plain (semisweet) and milk chocolate

175g/6oz/¾ cup unsalted (sweet) butter

75g/3oz/⅔ cup self-raising (self-rising) flour

3 large (US extra large) eggs

Rich Chocolate Biscuit Slice

This dark chocolate refrigerator cake is packed with crisp biscuit pieces and chunks of white chocolate for colour and flavour contrast. The slice is perfect served with strong coffee, either as a teatime treat or in place of dessert. Once set, cut the cake into slices and store the slices in an airtight container in the refrigerator until ready to serve.

SERVES EIGHT TO TEN

275g/10oz fruit and nut plain (semisweet) chocolate

130g/4½oz/ 9 tbsp unsalted (sweet) butter

90g/3½oz digestive biscuits (graham crackers)

90g/3½oz white chocolate

1 Grease and line the base and sides of a 450g/1lb loaf tin (pan) with baking parchment. Break the fruit and nut chocolate into pieces and place in a heatproof bowl with the butter. Place the bowl over a pan of barely simmering water and stir the chocolate gently until it is melted and smooth. Remove the bowl from the pan and leave to cool for 20 minutes.

2 Break the biscuits into small pieces. Finely chop the white chocolate. Stir the biscuits and white chocolate into the melted mixture until evenly combined. Turn the mixture into the prepared tin and pack down gently. Chill for about 2 hours, or until set. Cut the mixture into slices.

Cinnamon Pinwheels

These impressive sweet pastries go well with tea or coffee or as an accompaniment to ice cream and creamy desserts. If you find they turn soft during storage, re-crisp them briefly in the oven. Cinnamon is widely used in both sweet and savoury cooking: here ground cinnamon is used but it is also available as woody sticks. It has a delicious fragrant aroma and gives these simple-to-make pinwheels a warm spicy flavour.

MAKES TWENTY TO TWENTY-FOUR

50g/2oz/¼ cup caster (superfine) sugar, plus a little extra for sprinkling

10ml/2 tsp ground cinnamon

250g/9oz puff pastry

beaten egg, to glaze

1 Preheat the oven to 220°C/425°F/Gas 7. Grease a large baking sheet. Mix the sugar with the cinnamon in a small bowl.

2 Roll out the pastry on a lightly floured surface to a 20cm/8in square and sprinkle with half the sugar mixture. Roll out the pastry to a 25cm/10in square so that the sugar is pressed into it.

3 Brush with the beaten egg and then sprinkle with the remaining sugar mixture. Loosely roll up the pastry into a log, brushing the end of the pastry with a little more egg to secure the edge in place.

4 Using a sharp knife, cut the log into thin slices and transfer them to the prepared baking sheet. Bake for 10 minutes, until golden and crisp. Sprinkle with more sugar and transfer to a wire rack to cool.

Almond Cigars

These simple, Moroccan-inspired pastries can be prepared in minutes. They are perfect served with strong black coffee or black tea, or as an after-dinner treat. They are also delicious served with traditional sweet Moroccan mint tea. To serve, the pastries look very pretty sprinkled with a little icing (confectioners') sugar as a simple finishing touch.

250g/9oz marzipan

1 egg, lightly beaten

8–12 sheets filo pastry

melted butter, for brushing

MAKES EIGHT TO TWELVE

1 Knead the marzipan until soft and pliable, then put it in a mixing bowl and mix in the lightly beaten egg. Chill in the refrigerator for 1–2 hours.

2 Preheat the oven to 190°C/375°F/Gas 5. Lightly grease a baking sheet. Place a sheet of filo pastry on a piece of greaseproof (waxed) paper, keeping the remaining pastry covered with a damp cloth, and brush with the melted butter.

3 Shape 30–45ml/2–3 tbsp of the almond paste into a cylinder and place at one end of the pastry. Fold the pastry over to enclose the ends of the paste, then roll up to form a cigar shape. Place on the baking sheet and make 7–11 more cigars in the same way.

4 Bake the pastries in the preheated oven for about 15 minutes, or until golden brown in colour. Transfer to a wire rack to cool before serving.

All Butter Cookies

Crisp, buttery cookies are perfect with strawberries and cream or any creamy dessert or fruit compote. These biscuits or cookies are known as refrigerator biscuits as the mixture is chilled until it is firm enough to cut neatly into thin biscuits. The dough can be frozen and when thawed enough to slice, can be freshly baked, but do allow a little extra cooking time.

MAKES TWENTY-EIGHT TO THIRTY

1 Put the flour in a food processor. Add the butter and process until the mixture resembles coarse breadcrumbs. Add the icing sugar and vanilla, and process until the mixture comes together to form a dough. Knead lightly and shape into a thick sausage, 30cm/12in long and 5cm/2in in diameter. Wrap and chill for at least 1 hour, until firm.

2 Preheat the oven to 200°C/400°F/Gas 6. Grease two baking sheets. Using a sharp knife, cut 5mm/¼in thick slices from the dough and space them slightly apart on the baking sheet.

3 Bake for 8–10 minutes, alternating the position of the baking sheets in the oven halfway through cooking, if necessary, until the biscuits are cooked evenly and have just turned pale golden around the edges. Leave for 5 minutes, then transfer to a wire rack to cool. Serve dusted with icing sugar.

275g/10oz/2½ cups plain (all-purpose) flour

200g/7oz/scant 1 cup unsalted (sweet) butter

90g/3½oz/scant 1 cup icing (confectioners') sugar, plus extra for dusting

10ml/2 tsp vanilla essence (extract)

Almond Cookies

These short, light cookies have a melt-in-the-mouth texture. Their simplicity means they are endlessly versatile – irresistible with tea or coffee and stylish with special desserts.

MAKES ABOUT TWENTY-FOUR

115g/4oz/1 cup plain (all-purpose) flour

175g/6oz/1½ cups icing (confectioners') sugar, plus extra for dusting

50g/2oz/½ cup chopped almonds, plus halved almonds to decorate

115g/4oz/½ cup unsalted (sweet) butter, softened

COOK'S TIP *Use different-shaped cutters to make these cookies look even more interesting. Hearts, stars and crescents are three shapes that you might like to try.*

1 Preheat the oven to 180°C/350°F/Gas 4. Combine the flour, sugar and chopped almonds in a bowl.

2 Put the softened unsalted butter in the centre of the flour and nut mixture and use a blunt knife or your fingertips to draw the dry ingredients into the butter until a dough is formed. Shape the dough into a ball.

3 Place the dough on a lightly floured surface and roll it out to a thickness of about 3mm/⅛in. Using a 7.5cm/3in cookie cutter, cut out about 24 rounds, re-rolling the dough as necessary. Place the cookie rounds on baking sheets, leaving a little space between them. Bake the cookies for about 25 minutes, until pale golden.

4 Leave the cookies on the baking sheet for 10 minutes, then transfer to wire racks to cool. Dust thickly with sifted icing sugar before serving, decorated with halved almonds.

Golden Ginger Macaroons

Macaroons are classic no-fuss biscuits – easy to whisk up in minutes from the minimum ingredients and always acceptable. A hint of ginger makes this recipe that bit different. For a darker colour and slightly richer flavour, use soft dark brown sugar instead. Bake these biscuits on non-stick baking trays or on a baking tray lined with baking parchment to prevent them from sticking.

MAKES EIGHTEEN TO TWENTY

1 Preheat the oven to 180°C/350°F/Gas 4. In a large, grease-free bowl, whisk the egg white until stiff and standing in peaks, but not dry and crumbly, then whisk in the brown sugar.

2 Sprinkle the ground almonds and ginger over the whisked egg white and gently fold them together.

3 Using two teaspoons, place spoonfuls of the mixture on baking trays, leaving plenty of space between each. Bake for about 20 minutes, until pale golden brown and just turning crisp.

4 Leave to cool slightly on the baking trays before transferring to a wire rack to cool completely.

1 egg white

75g/3oz/scant ½ cup soft light brown sugar

115g/4oz/1 cup ground almonds

5ml/1 tsp ground ginger

VARIATION Other ground nuts, such as hazelnuts or walnuts, are good alternatives to the almonds. Ground cinnamon or mixed (apple pie) spice can be used instead of the ginger, if liked.

Nutty Nougat

Nougat is an almost magical sweetmeat that emerges from honey-flavoured meringue made with boiled syrup. Since any other nuts or candied fruits can be used instead of almonds, as long as you have eggs, sugar and honey, you have the potential for making an impromptu gift or dinner-party treat.

MAKES ABOUT 500G/1¼ LB

1 Line a 17.5cm/7in square cake tin (pan) with rice paper. Place the sugar, honey or syrup and 60ml/4 tbsp water in a large, heavy pan and heat gently, stirring frequently, until the sugar has completely dissolved.

2 Bring the syrup to the boil and boil gently to the soft crack stage (when the syrup dropped into cold water separates into hard but not brittle threads) or 151°C/304°F on a sugar thermometer.

3 Meanwhile, whisk the egg white until very stiff, but not crumbly, then slowly drizzle in the syrup while whisking constantly.

4 Quickly stir in the nuts and pour the mixture into the prepared tin. Leave to cool but, before the nougat becomes too hard, cut it into squares. Store in an airtight container.

225g/8oz/generous 1 cup granulated sugar

225g/8oz/1 cup clear honey or golden (light corn) syrup

1 large (US extra large) egg white

115g/4oz/1 cup flaked (sliced) almonds or chopped pistachio nuts, roasted

Stuffed Prunes

Prunes and plain chocolate are delectable partners, especially when the dried fruit is soaked in Armagnac. Serve these sophisticated sweetmeats dusted with cocoa powder as a dinner-party treat with coffee.

MAKES ABOUT THIRTY

1 Put the prunes in a bowl and pour the Armagnac over. Stir, then cover with clear film (plastic wrap) and set aside for 2 hours, or until the prunes have absorbed the liquid.

2 Make a slit along each prune to remove the stone (pit), making a hollow for the filling, but leaving the fruit intact.

3 Heat the cream in a pan almost to boiling point. Put 115g/4oz of the chocolate in a bowl and pour over the hot cream.

4 Stir until the chocolate has melted and the mixture is smooth. Leave to cool, until it has the consistency of softened butter.

5 Fill a piping (pastry) bag with a small plain nozzle with the chocolate mixture. Pipe into the cavities of the prunes. Chill for about 20 minutes.

6 Melt the remaining chocolate in a heatproof bowl set over a pan of barely simmering water. Using a fork, dip the prunes, one at a time, into the chocolate to coat them generously. Place on baking parchment to set.

**225g/8oz/
1 cup unpitted prunes**

**50ml/2fl oz/
¼ cup Armagnac**

**150ml/¼ pint/⅔ cup
double (heavy) cream**

**350g/12oz plain
(semisweet) chocolate,
broken into squares**

COOK'S TIP
Armagnac is a type of French brandy produced in the Pays de Gascogne in the south-west of the country. It has a pale colour and a biscuity aroma. Other types of brandy can be used in this recipe.

Chocolate Truffles

Luxurious truffles are expensive to buy but very easy and fun to make. These rich melt-in-the-mouth treats are flavoured with coffee liqueur, but you could use whisky or brandy instead. The mixture can be rolled in cocoa powder or icing (confectioners') sugar instead of being dipped in melted chocolate. Remember to store the fresh-cream truffles in the refrigerator.

MAKES TWENTY-FOUR

1 Melt 225g/8oz of the plain chocolate in a heatproof bowl set over a pan of barely simmering water. Stir in the cream and liqueur, then chill the mixture for 4 hours, until firm.

2 Divide the mixture into 24 equal pieces and quickly roll each into a ball. Chill for about 1 hour, or until the truffles are firm again.

3 Melt the remaining plain, white or milk chocolate in separate small bowls. Using two forks, carefully dip eight of the truffles, one at a time, into the melted plain chocolate.

4 Repeat to cover the remaining 16 truffles with the melted white or milk chocolate. Place the truffles on a board or tray, covered with wax paper or foil. Leave to set before placing in individual mini paper cases or transferring to a serving dish.

350g/12oz plain (semisweet) chocolate

75ml/5 tbsp double (heavy) cream

30ml/2 tbsp coffee liqueur, such as Tia Maria, Kahlúa or Toussaint

225g/8oz good quality white or milk dessert chocolate

EXTRAS

Ring the changes by adding one of the following to the mixture:

GINGER
Stir in 40g/1½ oz/¼ cup finely chopped crystallized ginger.

CANDIED FRUIT
Stir in 50g/2oz/⅓ cup finely chopped candied fruit, such as pineapple and orange.

PISTACHIOS
Stir in 25g/1oz/¼ cup chopped skinned pistachio nuts.

HAZELNUTS
Roll each ball of chilled truffle mixture around a whole skinned hazelnut.

Breads

THERE ARE FEW FOODS SO DELICIOUS AND COMFORTING

AS FRESHLY BAKED BREAD. THREE BASIC INGREDIENTS —

FLOUR, SALT AND YEAST — MIXED WITH WATER ARE ALL

THAT IS NEEDED TO MAKE A BASIC LOAF, WHILE THE

ADDITION OF A FOURTH INGREDIENT SUCH AS HERBS,

SUN-DRIED TOMATOES, OLIVE OIL OR MILK CAN

CREATE WONDERFUL, ENTICING VARIATIONS.

Granary Cob

Mixing and shaping a simple round loaf is one of the most satisfying kitchen activities and the result is incomparably excellent. This bread is made with fresh yeast – it is a similar colour and texture to putty and should crumble easily when broken. For best results, buy fresh yeast in small quantities as required: it will keep for up to one month in the refrigerator.

450g/1lb/4 cups Granary (multigrain) or malthouse flour

12.5ml/2½ tsp salt

15g/½oz fresh yeast

wheat flakes or cracked wheat, for sprinkling

MAKES ONE ROUND LOAF

1 Lightly flour a baking sheet. Mix the flour and 10ml/2 tsp of the salt together in a large bowl and make a well in the centre. Place in a very low oven for 5 minutes to warm.

2 Measure 300ml/½pint/1¼ cups lukewarm water. Mix the yeast with a little of the water, then blend in the rest. Pour the yeast mixture into the centre of the flour and mix to a dough.

3 Turn out on to a lightly floured surface and knead for about 10 minutes, until smooth and elastic. Place in a lightly oiled bowl, cover with lightly oiled clear film (plastic wrap) and leave to rise in a warm place for 1¼ hours, or until doubled in bulk.

4 Turn the dough out on to a lightly floured surface and knock back (punch down). Knead for 2–3 minutes, then roll into a ball. Place in the centre of the prepared baking sheet. Cover with an inverted bowl and leave to rise in a warm place for 30–45 minutes.

5 Preheat the oven to 230°C/450°F/Gas 8 towards the end of the rising time. Mix 30ml/2 tbsp water with the remaining salt and brush evenly over the bread. Sprinkle the loaf with wheat flakes or cracked wheat.

6 Bake the bread for 15 minutes, then reduce the oven temperature to 200°C/400°F/Gas 6 and bake for a further 20 minutes, or until the loaf is firm to the touch and sounds hollow when tapped on the base. Cool on a wire rack.

Grant Loaves

This quick and easy recipe was created by a baker called Doris Grant and was published in the 1940s. It is a dream for busy cooks as the dough requires no kneading and takes only a minute to mix. Nowadays we can make the recipe even quicker by using easy-blend yeast, which is added directly to the dry ingredients.

MAKES THREE LOAVES

1 Thoroughly grease three loaf tins (pans), each 21 x 11 x 6cm/ 8½ x 4½ x 2½in and set aside in a warm place. Sift the flour and salt together in a large bowl and warm slightly to take off the chill.

2 Sprinkle the dried yeast over 150ml/¼ pint/⅔ cup lukewarm water. After a couple of minutes, stir in the muscovado sugar. Leave the mixture for 10 minutes.

3 Make a well in the centre of the flour. Pour in the yeast mixture and add a further 900ml/1½ pints/3¾ cups lukewarm water. Stir to form a slippery dough. Mix for about 1 minute, working the dry ingredients from the sides into the middle.

4 Divide among the prepared tins, cover with oiled clear film (plastic wrap) and leave to rise in a warm place for 30 minutes, or until the dough has risen by about one-third to within 1cm/ ½in of the top of the tins.

5 Meanwhile, preheat the oven to 200°C/400°F/Gas 6. Bake for 40 minutes, or until the loaves are crisp and sound hollow when tapped on the base. Turn out on to a wire rack to cool.

1.3kg/3lb/12 cups wholemeal (whole-wheat) bread flour

15ml/1 tbsp salt

15ml/1 tbsp easy-blend (rapid-rise) dried yeast

15ml/1 tbsp muscovado (molasses) sugar

Cottage Loaf

Create a culinary masterpiece from a few basic ingredients and experience the satisfaction of traditional baking. Serve this classic-shaped loaf to accompany home-made soup.

MAKES ONE LARGE ROUND LOAF

675g/1½lb/6 cups unbleached strong white bread flour

10ml/2 tsp salt

20g/¾oz fresh yeast

1 Lightly grease two baking sheets. Sift the flour and salt together into a large bowl and make a well in the centre.

2 Mix the yeast in 150ml/¼ pint/⅔ cup lukewarm water until dissolved. Pour into the centre of the flour and add a further 250ml/8fl oz/1 cup lukewarm water, then mix to a firm dough.

3 Knead the dough on a lightly floured surface for 10 minutes, until it is smooth and elastic. Place in a lightly oiled bowl, cover with lightly oiled clear film (plastic wrap) and leave to rise in a warm place for about 1 hour.

4 Turn out on to a lightly floured surface and knock back (punch down). Knead for 2–3 minutes, then divide the dough into two-thirds and one-third and shape each piece into a ball. Place the balls of dough on the prepared baking sheets. Cover with inverted bowls and leave to rise in a warm place for 30 minutes.

5 Gently flatten the top of the larger round of dough and cut a cross in the centre, about 4cm/1½in across. Brush with a little water and place the smaller round on top. Carefully press a hole through the middle of the top ball, down into the lower part, using your thumb and first two fingers. Cover with lightly oiled clear film and leave to rest in a warm place for about 10 minutes.

6 Preheat the oven to 220°C/425°F/Gas 7 and place the bread on the lower shelf of the oven. Bake for 35–40 minutes, or until a rich golden brown colour. Cool on a wire rack before serving.

Split Tin

The deep centre split down this loaf gives it its name. The split tin loaf slices well for making thick-cut sandwiches, or for serving hearty chunks of bread to accompany robust cheese.

MAKES ONE LOAF

500g/1¼lb/5 cups unbleached strong white bread flour, plus extra for dusting

10ml/2 tsp salt

15g/½oz fresh yeast

60ml/4 tbsp lukewarm milk

1 Grease a 900g/2lb loaf tin (pan). Sift the flour and salt into a bowl and make a well in the centre. Mix the yeast with 150ml/¼ pint/⅔ cup lukewarm water. Stir in another 150ml/¼ pint/⅔ cup lukewarm water. Pour the yeast mixture into the centre of the flour and using your fingers, mix in a little flour to form a smooth batter.

2 Sprinkle a little more flour from around the edge over the batter and leave in a warm place for about 20 minutes to "sponge". Add the milk and remaining flour; mix to a firm dough.

3 Place on a lightly floured surface and knead for about 10 minutes, until smooth and elastic. Place in a lightly oiled bowl, cover with lightly oiled clear film (plastic wrap) and leave to rise in a warm place for 1–1¼ hours, or until nearly doubled in bulk.

4 Knock back (punch down) the dough and turn out on to a lightly floured surface. Shape it into a rectangle, the length of the prepared tin. Roll the dough up lengthways, tuck the ends under and place, seam side down, in the tin. Cover the loaf and leave to rise in a warm place for about 20–30 minutes.

5 Using a sharp knife, make one deep central slash. Dust the top of the loaf with a little sieved flour. Leave for 10–15 minutes. Meanwhile, preheat the oven to 230°C/450°F/Gas 8. Bake for 15 minutes, then reduce the oven temperature to 200°C/400°F/Gas 6. Bake for 20–25 minutes, until golden and it sounds hollow when tapped on the base. Cool on a wire rack.

Poppy-seeded Bloomer

This long, crusty loaf gets its fabulous flavour from poppy seeds. Cut into thick slices, the bread is perfect for mopping up the cooking juices of hearty stews, or for absorbing good dressing on summery salads. A variety of seeds can be used to add flavour, texture and colour to this loaf – try sunflower, pumpkin or sesame seeds as an alternative to the poppy seeds. Brushing the loaf with the salted water before baking helps to give it a crisp, crusty finish.

MAKES ONE LARGE LOAF

1 Lightly grease a baking sheet. Sift the flour and 10ml/2 tsp salt together into a large bowl and make a well in the centre.

2 Measure 450ml/¾ pint/scant 2 cups lukewarm water and stir about a third of it into the yeast in a bowl. Stir in the remaining water and pour into the centre of the flour. Mix, gradually incorporating the surrounding flour, to a firm dough.

3 Turn out on to a lightly floured surface and knead the dough very well, for at least 10 minutes, until smooth and elastic. Place the dough in a lightly oiled bowl, cover with lightly oiled clear film (plastic wrap) and leave to rise, at cool room temperature (about 15–18°C/60–65°F), for 5–6 hours, or until doubled in bulk.

4 Knock back (punch down) the dough, turn out on to a lightly floured surface and knead it thoroughly for about 5 minutes. Return the dough to the bowl and re-cover. Leave to rise, at cool room temperature, for a further 2 hours or slightly longer.

5 Knock back again and repeat the thorough kneading. Leave the dough to rest for 5 minutes, then roll out on a lightly floured surface into a rectangle 2.5cm/1in thick. Roll the dough up from one long side and shape it into a square-ended, thick baton shape about 33 x 13cm/13 x 5in.

6 Place the loaf, seam side up, on a lightly floured baking sheet. Cover with lightly oiled clear film and leave to rest for 15 minutes. Turn the loaf over and place on the greased baking sheet. Plump the loaf up by tucking the dough under the sides and ends. Using a sharp knife, cut six diagonal slashes on the top.

7 Leave to rest, covered, in a warm place, for 10 minutes. Meanwhile, preheat the oven to 230°C/450°F/Gas 8.

8 Mix the remaining salt with 30ml/2 tbsp water and brush this glaze over the bread. Sprinkle with poppy seeds.

9 Spray the oven with water, bake the bread immediately for 20 minutes, then reduce the oven temperature to 200°C/400°F/Gas 6. Bake for 25 minutes more, or until golden and it sounds hollow when tapped on the base. Transfer to a wire rack to cool.

675g/1½lb/6 cups unbleached strong white bread flour

12.5ml/2½ tsp salt

15g/½oz fresh yeast

poppy seeds, for sprinkling

COOK'S TIP *The traditional cracked, crusty appearance of this loaf is difficult to achieve in a domestic oven. However, you can get a similar result by spraying the oven with water before baking. If the underneath of the loaf is not very crusty at the end of baking, turn it over on the baking sheet, switch off the heat and leave it in the oven for a further 5–10 minutes.*

French Baguette

Fine French flour is available from French delicatessens and superior supermarkets. If you cannot find any, try ordinary plain flour instead. Baguettes have a wide variety of uses: split horizontally and fill with meats, cheeses and salads; slice diagonally and toast the slices to serve with soup; or simply cut into chunks, spread with unsalted (sweet) butter and serve with French cheeses.

500g/1¼lb/5 cups unbleached strong white bread flour

115g/4oz/1 cup fine French plain (all-purpose) flour

10ml/2 tsp salt

15g/½oz fresh yeast

MAKES THREE LOAVES

1 Sift the flours and salt into a bowl. Add the yeast to 550ml/18fl oz/2½ cups lukewarm water in another bowl and stir. Gradually beat in half the flour mixture to form a batter. Cover with clear film (plastic wrap) and leave for about 3 hours, or until nearly trebled in size.

2 Add the remaining flour a little at a time, beating with your hand. Turn out on to a lightly floured surface and knead for 8–10 minutes to form a moist dough. Place in a lightly oiled bowl, cover with lightly oiled clear film and leave to rise, in a warm place, for about 1 hour.

3 Knock back (punch down) the dough, turn out on to a floured surface and divide into three equal pieces. Shape each into a ball and then into a 15 x 7.5cm/6 x 3in rectangle. Fold the bottom third up lengthways and the top third down and press down. Seal the edges. Repeat two or three more times until each loaf is an oblong. Leave to rest in between folding for a few minutes.

4 Gently stretch each piece of dough into a 33–35cm/13–14in long loaf. Pleat a floured dishtowel on a baking sheet to make three moulds for the loaves. Place the loaves between the pleats, cover with lightly oiled clear film and leave to rise in a warm place for 45–60 minutes.

5 Preheat the oven to maximum, at least 230°C/450°F/Gas 8. Roll the loaves on to a baking sheet, spaced well apart. Slash the top of each loaf diagonally several times. Place at the top of the oven, spray the inside of the oven with water and bake for 20–25 minutes.

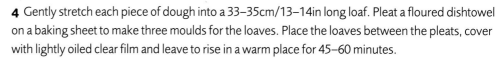

COOK'S TIP *Baguettes are difficult to reproduce at home as they require a very hot oven and steam. However, by using less yeast and a triple fermentation you can produce a bread with a superior taste and far better texture than mass-produced baguettes. It also helps if you spray the oven twice with water during the first 5 minutes of baking. These loaves are best eaten on the day of baking.*

Rosemary Focaccia

If you do not need both loaves, freeze one for another time and warm it in the oven before serving. Sprinkle the loaves with finely chopped garlic, if you prefer.

MAKES TWO LOAVES

1 Put the flour and yeast in a large bowl with 5ml/1 tsp salt. Stir in 45ml/3 tbsp of the oil and 450ml/¾ pint/scant 2 cups lukewarm water. Mix with a round-bladed knife, then by hand to a soft dough, adding a little more lukewarm water if the dough feels dry.

2 Turn the dough out on to a lightly floured surface and knead for 10 minutes, until smooth and elastic. Put in a lightly oiled bowl and cover with oiled clear film (plastic wrap). Leave in a warm place for about 1 hour, until doubled in size.

3 Preheat the oven to 200°C/400°F/Gas 6. Turn out the dough on to a floured surface and cut in half. Roll out each half into a 25cm/10in round. Transfer to greased baking sheets, cover with lightly oiled clear film and leave for 20 minutes, until risen.

4 Press your fingers into the dough to make deep holes all over it about 3cm/1¼in apart. Leave for a further 5 minutes. Sprinkle with the rosemary and plenty of sea salt. Sprinkle with water to keep the crust moist and bake for 25 minutes, until pale golden. Remove from the oven and drizzle with the remaining olive oil. Transfer to a wire rack to cool.

675g/1½lb/4 cups strong white bread flour

15ml/1 tbsp easy-blend (rapid-rise) dried yeast

75ml/5 tbsp olive oil

45ml/3 tbsp chopped fresh rosemary

Scottish Morning Rolls

These soft, spongy bread rolls are irresistible while still warm and aromatic. Made with milk, rather than the more usual water, they have a rich flavour. In Scotland they are a firm favourite for breakfast with fried eggs and bacon. To speed up the rising time, place the rolls in the airing cupboard or on the top of the preheated oven.

MAKES TEN ROLLS

1 Grease two baking sheets. Sift the flour and salt together into a large bowl and make a well in the centre. Mix the yeast with the milk, then mix in 150ml/¼ pint/⅔ cup lukewarm water. Add to the centre of the flour and mix together to form a soft dough.

2 Knead the dough lightly in the bowl, then cover with lightly oiled clear film (plastic wrap) and leave to rise in a warm place for 1 hour, or until doubled in bulk. Turn the dough out on to a lightly floured surface and knock back (punch down).

3 Divide the dough into ten equal pieces. Knead lightly and, using a rolling pin, shape each piece of dough into a flat oval 10 x 7.5cm/ 4 x 3in, or a flat round 9cm/3½in.

4 Transfer to the prepared baking sheets, spaced well apart, and cover the rolls with oiled clear film. Leave to rise, in a warm place, for about 30 minutes.

5 Meanwhile, preheat the oven to 200°C/400°F/Gas 6. Press each roll in the centre with the three middle fingers to equalize the air bubbles and to help prevent blistering. Brush with milk and dust with flour. Bake for 15–20 minutes, or until lightly browned. Dust with more flour and cool slightly on a wire rack. Serve warm.

450g/1lb/4 cups unbleached strong white bread flour, plus extra for dusting

10ml/2 tsp salt

20g/¾oz fresh yeast

150ml/¼ pint/⅔ cup lukewarm milk, plus extra for glazing

Panini all'Olio

Italian-style dough enriched and flavoured with extra virgin olive oil is versatile for making decorative rolls. Children will love helping to make and shape these rolls – they can try making twists, fingers or artichoke-shapes, or just about any shape they want. The rolls are sure to disappear as soon as they are cool enough to eat.

450g/1lb/4 cups unbleached strong white bread flour

10ml/2 tsp salt

15g/½ oz fresh yeast

60ml/4 tbsp extra virgin olive oil, plus extra for brushing

MAKES SIXTEEN ROLLS

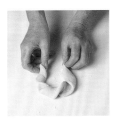

1 Lightly oil three baking sheets. Sift the flour and salt together in a large bowl and make a well in the centre. Measure 250ml/8fl oz/1 cup lukewarm water. Cream the yeast with half the water, then stir in the remainder. Add to the well with the oil and mix to a dough.

2 Turn the dough out on to a lightly floured surface and knead for 8–10 minutes, until smooth and elastic. Place in a lightly oiled bowl, cover with lightly oiled clear film (plastic wrap) and leave to rise in a warm place for about 1 hour, or until nearly doubled in bulk.

3 Turn the dough on to a lightly floured surface and knock back (punch down). Divide into 12 equal pieces and shape into rolls. To make twists, roll each piece of dough into a strip 30cm/12in long and 4cm/1½in wide. Twist each strip into a loose spiral and join the ends together to make a circle. Place on the baking sheets, spaced well apart. Brush lightly with olive oil, cover with lightly oiled clear film and leave to rise in a warm place for 20–30 minutes.

4 To make fingers, flatten each piece of dough into an oval and roll to about 23cm/9in long. Roll up from the wider end. Gently stretch the dough roll to 20–23cm/8–9in long. Cut in half. Place on the baking sheets, spaced well apart. Brush the dough with olive oil, cover with lightly oiled clear film and leave to rise in a warm place for 20–30 minutes.

5 To make artichoke-shapes, shape each piece of dough into a ball and space well apart on the baking sheets. Brush with oil, cover with lightly oiled clear film and leave to rise in a warm place for 20–30 minutes. Using scissors, snip 5mm/¼in deep cuts in a circle on the top of each ball, then make five larger horizontal cuts around the sides.

6 Preheat the oven to 200°C/400°F/Gas 6. Bake the rolls for 15 minutes.

Pitta Bread

Soft, slightly bubbly pitta bread is a pleasure to make. It can be eaten in a variety of ways, such as Mediterranean-style filled with salad or little chunks of meat cooked on the barbecue, or it can be torn into pieces and dipped in savoury dips such as hummus or tzatziki. Chop any leftover bread and incorporate into the Lebanese salad *fattoush* with parsley, mint, tomatoes and cucumber.

MAKES TWELVE

500g/1¼lb/5 cups strong white bread flour, or half white and half wholemeal (whole-wheat)

12.5ml/2½ tsp easy-blend (rapid-rise) dried yeast

15ml/1 tbsp salt

15ml/1 tbsp olive oil

1 Combine the flour, yeast and salt. Combine the oil and 250ml/8fl oz/1 cup water, then add half of the flour mixture, stirring in the same direction, until the dough is stiff. Knead in the remaining flour. Place the dough in a clean bowl, cover with a clean dishtowel and leave in a warm place for at least 30 minutes and up to 2 hours.

2 Knead the dough for 10 minutes, or until smooth. Lightly oil the bowl, place the dough in it, cover again and leave to rise in a warm place for about 1 hour, or until doubled in size.

3 Divide the dough into 12 equal pieces. With lightly floured hands, flatten each piece, then roll out into a round measuring about 20cm/8in and about 4mm–1cm/¼–½in thick. Keep the rolled breads covered while you make the remaining pittas.

4 Heat a heavy frying pan over a medium-high heat. When hot, lay one piece of flattened dough in the pan and cook for 15–20 seconds. Turn it over and cook the second side for about 1 minute.

5 When large bubbles start to form on the bread, turn it over again. It should puff up. Using a clean dishtowel, gently press on the bread where the bubbles have formed. Cook for a total of 3 minutes, then remove the pitta from the pan. Repeat with the remaining dough. Wrap the pitta breads in a clean dishtowel, stacking them as each one is cooked. Serve the pittas hot while they are soft and moist.

VARIATION To bake the breads, preheat the oven to 220°C/425°F/Gas 7. Fill an unglazed or partially glazed dish with hot water and place in the bottom of the hot oven. Alternatively, arrange a handful of unglazed tiles in the base of the oven. Use either a non-stick baking sheet or a lightly oiled baking sheet and heat in the oven for a few minutes. Place two or three pieces of flattened dough on to the hot baking sheet and place in the hottest part of the oven. Bake for 2–3 minutes until puffed up. Repeat with the remaining dough.

Yemeni Sponge Flat Breads

These flat breads, known as *lahuhs* and made from a batter, are bubbly and soft. They are eaten with soups but are also good with salads, dips or cheese.

SERVES FOUR

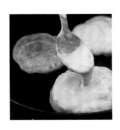

1 Measure 500ml/17fl oz/generous 2 cups lukewarm water. In a bowl, dissolve the dried yeast in about 75ml/5 tbsp of the water. Leave in a warm place for about 10 minutes, or until frothy.

2 Stir the remaining water, the flour, salt and melted butter or vegetable oil into the yeast mixture and mix until it forms a smooth batter. Cover with a clean dishtowel, then leave in a warm place for about 1 hour, until doubled in size.

3 Stir the thick, frothy batter and, if it seems too thick to ladle out, add a little extra water. Cover and leave the batter to stand in a warm place for about 1 hour.

4 Cook the flat breads in a non-stick frying pan. Ladle 45–60ml/ 3–4 tbsp of batter (or less for smaller breads) into the pan and cook over a low heat until the top is bubbling and the colour has changed. (Traditionally these breads are cooked on only one side, but they can be turned over and the second side cooked for just a moment, if you like.)

5 Remove the cooked flat bread from the frying pan with a spatula and keep warm in a clean dishtowel. Continue cooking until you have used up all the remaining batter.

15ml/1 tbsp dried active yeast

350g/12oz/ 3 cups plain (all-purpose) flour

5ml/1 tsp salt

50g/2oz/¼ cup butter, melted, or 60ml/4 tbsp vegetable oil

COOK'S TIP *Use two or three frying pans at the same time so that the flat breads are ready together and so can be eaten piping hot.*

West Indian Flat Breads

Eclectic Caribbean food is influenced by a wide range of international cultures. It is the Anglo-Indian connection that brought the Indian flat bread called roti to Trinidad in the West Indies. Serve these simple-to-make breads straight from the pan to accompany spicy seafood chowders, curries, or any other dish that has plenty of sauce for mopping up.

MAKES EIGHT ROTIS

1 Mix the flour, baking powder and salt together in a large bowl and make a well in the centre. Gradually mix in 300ml/½ pint/1¼ cups water to make a firm dough.

2 Knead on a lightly floured surface until smooth. Place in a lightly oiled bowl, cover with lightly oiled clear film (plastic wrap). Leave to stand for 20 minutes.

3 Divide the dough into eight equal pieces and roll each one on a lightly floured surface into an 18cm/7in round. Brush the surface of each round with a little of the clarified butter or ghee, fold in half and half again. Cover the folded rounds with lightly oiled clear film (plastic wrap) and leave for 10 minutes.

4 Take one roti and roll out on a lightly floured surface into a round about 20–23cm/8–9in in diameter. Brush both sides with some clarified butter or ghee.

5 Heat a griddle or heavy frying pan, add the roti and cook for about 1 minute. Turn over and cook for 2 minutes, then turn over again and cook for 1 minute. Wrap in a clean dishtowel to keep warm while cooking the remaining rotis. Serve warm.

450g/1lb/4 cups atta or fine wholemeal (whole-wheat) flour

5ml/1 tsp baking powder

5ml/1 tsp salt

115–150g/4–5oz/8–10 tbsp clarified butter or ghee, melted

Tandoori Rotis

Indian flat breads are fun to make at home: these may not be strictly authentic in terms of cooking method, but they taste fantastic. This bread would normally be baked in a tandoor, a clay oven that is heated with charcoal or wood. The oven becomes extremely hot, cooking the bread in minutes. The rotis are ready when light brown bubbles appear on the surface.

MAKES SIX ROTIS

350g/12oz/3 cups atta or fine wholemeal (whole-wheat) flour

5ml/1 tsp salt

30–45ml/2–3 tbsp melted ghee or butter, for brushing

1 Sift the flour and salt into a large bowl. Add 250ml/8fl oz/1 cup water and mix to a soft dough. Knead on a lightly floured surface for 3–4 minutes, until smooth. Place the dough in a lightly oiled mixing bowl, cover with lightly oiled clear film (plastic wrap) and leave to rest for 1 hour.

2 Turn out on to a lightly floured surface. Divide the dough into six pieces and shape each piece into a ball. Press out into a larger round with the palm of your hand, cover with lightly oiled clear film (plastic wrap) and leave to rest for 10 minutes.

3 Meanwhile, preheat the oven to 230°C/450°F/Gas 8. Place three baking sheets in the oven to heat. Roll the rotis into 15cm/6in rounds, place two on each baking sheet and bake for 8–10 minutes. Brush with ghee or butter and serve warm.

Preserves, Pickles, Relishes and Sauces

SWEET AND SAVOURY PRESERVES, CONDIMENTS AND
SAUCES CAN ADD THE FINISHING TOUCH TO A SIMPLE DISH.
A SPOONFUL OF FRUIT JAM OR JELLY CAN TRANSFORM A
PLAIN SCONE INTO TEATIME TREAT, WHILE PIQUANT PICKLES
AND RELISHES CAN ENLIVEN BREAD AND CHEESE, AND A
FLAVOURSOME SAUCE CAN TURN SIMPLY COOKED FISH
INTO A REALLY SPECIAL MEAL.

Bramble Jelly

The tart, fruity flavour of wild blackberries makes this jelly one of the best, especially for serving with hot buttered toast or English muffins. When picking the fruit, include a small proportion of red unripe berries for a good set. Redcurrant jelly is made in the same way, but with less sugar. Reduce the quantity to 350g/12oz/1½ cups of sugar for every 600ml/ 1 pint/2½ cups of fruit juice.

900g/2lb/ 8 cups blackberries

juice of 1 lemon

about 900g/2lb/ 4 cups caster (superfine) sugar

MAKES 900G/2LB

1 Put the blackberries and lemon juice into a large pan (use a preserving pan with two handles if possible). Add 300ml/½ pint/1¼ cups water. Cover the pan and cook for 15–30 minutes, or until the blackberries are very soft.

2 Ladle into a jelly bag or a large sieve lined with muslin (cheesecloth) and set over a large mixing bowl. Leave the fruit to drip overnight to obtain the maximum amount of juice. Do not disturb or squeeze the bag or the jelly will be cloudy.

3 Discard the fruit pulp. Measure the juice and allow 450g/1lb/2 cups sugar to every 600ml/ 1 pint/2½ cups juice. Place the juice and sugar in a large, heavy pan and bring to the boil, stirring constantly until the sugar has dissolved.

4 Boil the mixture rapidly until the jelly registers 105°C/220°F on a sugar thermometer, or test for setting by spooning a small amount on to a chilled saucer (keep a saucer in the freezer for this purpose). Chill for 3 minutes, then push the mixture with your finger: if wrinkles form on the surface of the jelly, it is ready.

5 Skim off any scum and immediately pour the jelly into warm sterilized jars. Cover and seal immediately, then label when the jars are cold.

Strawberry Jam

This is the classic fragrant preserve for English afternoon tea, served with freshly baked scones and clotted cream. It is also extremely good stirred into plain yogurt for breakfast. When choosing strawberries for making jam, pick undamaged, slightly under-ripe fruit if possible – the pectin content will be high and ensure a good set.

MAKES ABOUT 1.3KG/3LB

1kg/2¼lb/8 cups small strawberries

900g/2lb/4 cups granulated sugar

juice of 2 lemons

1 Layer the strawberries and sugar in a large bowl. Cover and leave overnight.

2 The next day, scrape the strawberries and their juice into a large, heavy pan. Add the lemon juice. Gradually bring to the boil over a low heat, stirring until the sugar has dissolved.

3 Boil steadily for 10–15 minutes, or until the jam registers 105°C/220°F on a sugar thermometer. Alternatively, test for setting by spooning a small amount on to a chilled saucer. Chill for 3 minutes, then push the jam with your finger: if wrinkles form on the surface, it is ready. Cool for 10 minutes.

4 Stir the jam before pouring it into warm sterilized jars, filling them right to the top. Cover with waxed paper discs immediately, but do not seal with lids until the jam is completely cold.

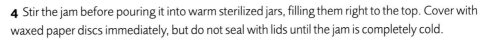

COOK'S TIP
For best results when making jam, don't wash the strawberries unless absolutely necessary. Instead, brush off any dirt, or wipe the strawberries with a damp cloth. If you have to wash any, pat them dry and then spread them out on a clean dishtowel to dry.

Spiced Poached Kumquats

Warm cinnamon and star anise make a heady combination with the full citrus flavour of kumquats. Star anise is an attractive spice: it is an eight-pointed star that contains tiny aniseed-flavoured, amber coloured seeds. The kumquats go well with rich meats, such as roast pork or baked ham, or with punchy goat's milk cheese. They are also good with desserts and ice creams.

SERVES SIX

1 Cut the kumquats in half and discard the pips (seeds). Place the kumquats in a pan with the caster sugar, 150ml/¼ pint/⅔ cup water and the cinnamon stick and star anise. Cook over a gentle heat, stirring until the sugar has dissolved.

2 Increase the heat, cover the pan and boil the mixture for about 8–10 minutes, until the kumquats are tender. To bottle the kumquats, spoon them into warm, sterilized jars, seal and label.

3 If you want to serve the spiced kumquats soon after making them, let the mixture cool, then chill it.

450g/1lb/ 4 cups kumquats

115g/4oz/ ½ cup caster (superfine) sugar

1 small cinnamon stick

1 star anise

Three-fruit Marmalade

Bitter marmalade oranges have a powerful flavour and plenty of setting power to make an excellent preserve. Known as Seville oranges, they are usually only available for a short time in January – but sweet oranges can be used in this recipe if necessary.

MAKES 2.25KG/5LB

1 Wash the fruit, halve, and squeeze their juice. Pour into a large heavy pan or preserving pan. Tip the pips (seeds) and pulp into a square of muslin (cheesecloth), gather the sides into a bag and tie the neck. Tie the bag to the pan handle so that it dangles in the juice.

2 Remove and discard the membranes and pith from the citrus skins and cut the rinds into slivers. Add to the pan with 1.75 litres/3 pints/7½ cups water. Heat until simmering and then cook gently for 2 hours. Test the rinds for softness by pressing a cooled piece with a finger.

3 Lift out the muslin bag, squeezing out the juice into the pan. Discard the bag. Stir the sugar into the pan and heat very gently, stirring occasionally, until the sugar has dissolved.

4 Bring the mixture to the boil and boil for 10–15 minutes, or until the marmalade registers 105°C/220°F on a sugar thermometer. Alternatively, test the marmalade for setting by pouring a small amount on to a chilled saucer. Chill for 3 minutes, then push the marmalade with your finger: if wrinkles form on the surface, it is ready. Cool for 15 minutes.

5 Stir the marmalade and pour it into warm, sterilized jars. Cover with waxed paper discs. Seal and label when completely cold. Store in a cool dark cupboard.

2 Seville (Temple) oranges

2 lemons

1 grapefruit

1.5kg/3lb 6oz/ 6¾ cups granulated sugar

COOK'S TIP *Allow the marmalade to cool slightly before potting so that it is thick enough to stop the fruit from sinking in the jars.*

Preserved Lemons

These are widely used in Middle Eastern cooking, for which only the peel is used and not the pulp. In this recipe the lemons are cut into wedges instead of being preserved whole, in traditional style. The wedges are more practical for potting and they are also easy to prepare before use.

MAKES TWO JARS

1 Wash the lemons well and cut each into six to eight wedges. Press a generous amount of sea salt into the cut surfaces, pushing it into every crevice.

2 Pack the salted lemon wedges into two 1.2 litre/2 pint/5 cup sterilized jars. To each jar, add 30–45ml/2–3 tbsp salt and 90ml/6 tbsp lemon juice, then top up with boiling water to cover the lemons. (If using larger jars, use more lemon juice and less water.)

3 Cover the jars and leave to stand for 2–4 weeks before serving.

4 To serve, rinse the preserved lemons well to remove some of the salty flavour, then pull off and discard the flesh. Cut the lemon peel into strips or leave in chunks and use as you like.

10 unwaxed lemons

sea salt

about 200ml/ 7fl oz/scant 1 cup fresh lemon juice or a combination of fresh and preserved

Middle Eastern Pickle

Beetroot brings attractive colour and its inimitable sweet, slightly earthy flavour to this Middle Eastern speciality. The pickle is delicious with falafel or cold roast beef. When buying beetroot, choose firm, unblemished, small- to medium-sized specimens. If you buy beetroot with green tops, reserve them and cook like spinach for a tasty vegetable accompaniment.

MAKES FOUR JARS

**1kg/2¼lb
young turnips**

**3–4 raw
beetroot (beets)**

**about 45ml/3 tbsp
kosher salt or
coarse sea salt**

juice of 1 lemon

1 Wash, but do not peel the turnips and beetroot. Then cut them into slices about 5mm/¼ in thick. Put the salt in a bowl with about 1.5 litres/2½ pints/6¼ cups water, stir and leave on one side until the salt has completely dissolved.

2 Sprinkle the beetroot with lemon juice and divide among four 1.2 litre/2 pint/5 cup sterilized jars. Top with the sliced turnips, packing them in very tightly. Pour over the brine, making sure that the vegetables are completely covered.

3 Seal the jars and leave in a cool place for seven days for the flavours to develop before serving.

Horseradish and Beetroot Sauce

This is a traditional Jewish speciality. Known as chrain, it is often eaten at Pesah, the Passover meal, for which horseradish is one of the traditional bitter flavours. However, it complements a variety of foods and dishes of many different cooking styles, including roast meats and grilled fish.

SERVES ABOUT EIGHT

150g/5oz grated fresh horseradish

2 cooked beetroot (beets), grated

about 15ml/ 1 tbsp sugar

15–30ml/1–2 tbsp red wine vinegar

1 Put the horseradish and beetroot in a bowl and mix together, then season with sugar, vinegar and salt to taste.

2 Spoon the sauce into a sterilized jar, packing it down firmly, and seal. Store in the refrigerator, where it will keep for up to 2 weeks.

COOK'S TIP *Fresh horseradish is very potent and should be handled with care as it can make the skin burn as well as the eyes run. Wear fine rubber gloves to protect your hands and always work in a well-ventilated kitchen.*

Yellow Pepper and Coriander Relish

Relishes are quick and easy to make and they are delicious with cold meats and cheese or as a sandwich filler. Here the ingredients are lightly cooked, then processed to a chunky consistency. Red or orange (bell) peppers will work just as well as yellow as they all have a sweet flavour. Don't use green peppers though, because they are not sweet.

SERVES FOUR TO SIX

1 Seed and coarsely chop the peppers. Heat the oil in a frying pan and gently cook the peppers, stirring frequently, for 8–10 minutes, until lightly coloured.

2 Meanwhile, seed the chilli and slice it as thinly as possible. Transfer the peppers and cooking juices to a food processor and process lightly until chopped. Transfer half the peppers to a bowl. Using a sharp knife, chop the fresh coriander, then add to the food processor and process briefly.

3 Tip the contents of the food processor into the bowl with the rest of the peppers and add the chilli and salt. Mix well, cover and chill until ready to serve.

3 large yellow (bell) peppers

45ml/3 tbsp sesame oil

1 large mild fresh red chilli

small handful of fresh coriander (cilantro)

COOK'S TIP *Other flavoured oils, such as lemon- or garlic-infused oil, can be used in place of the sesame oil. The relish can be stored in an airtight container in the refrigerator for several days.*

Hot Mango Salsa

For sweet, tangy results, select a really juicy, ripe mango for this salsa – it is not worth making the salsa with a firm, unripe mango as it will not taste as good as it should. Keep an unripe mango in the fruit bowl for a few days until it has ripened. This fruity salsa is a delicious accompaniment to chargrilled or barbecued chicken or fish.

SERVES FOUR TO SIX

1 To prepare the mango, cut the flesh off on either side of the flat stone (pit). Peel and finely dice the mango halves and cut off and chop the flesh that still clings to the stone.

2 Finely grate the lime rind and squeeze the juice. Seed and finely shred the fresh red chilli.

3 Finely chop the onion and mix it in a bowl with the mango, lime rind, 15ml/1 tbsp lime juice, the chilli and a little salt. Cover and chill until ready to serve.

1 medium ripe mango

1 lime

1 large mild fresh red chilli

½ small red onion

Harissa

This simplified version of harissa – the classic spicy North African sauce – is extremely quick to make. It can be served as a dip with wedges of Middle Eastern flat bread, as a condiment with couscous and other North African dishes, or as a flavouring to spice up meat and vegetable stews. This basic spice blend goes very well with other aromatic herbs and spices so you can vary the flavour by adding chopped fresh coriander (cilantro) or a pinch of caraway seeds along with the lemon juice, if you like.

SERVES FOUR TO SIX

1 Put the paprika, cayenne pepper, ground cumin and 250ml/8fl oz/ 1 cup water in a large, heavy pan and season with salt to taste.

2 Bring the spice mixture to the boil, then immediately remove the pan from the heat.

3 Stir in the lemon juice to taste and allow to cool completely before serving or using.

45ml/3 tbsp paprika

2.5–5ml/½–1 tsp cayenne pepper

1.5ml/¼ tsp ground cumin

juice of ¼–½ lemon

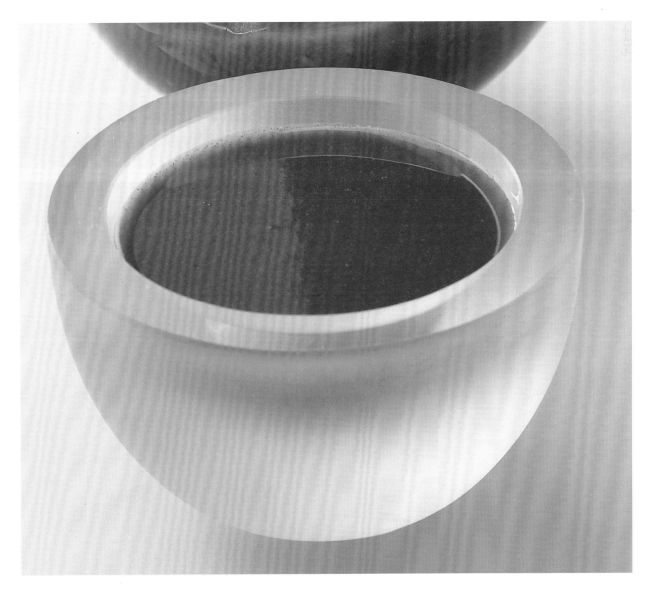

Aioli

This classic, creamy garlic mayonnaise from France is simple to make and absolutely delicious. Serve it with salads or as a dip with crudités, with potato wedges, or as a quick sauce for pan-fried salmon. Try to use extra virgin olive oil for this mayonnaise if you can – it has a rich and delicious flavour that really makes this sauce special.

SERVES FOUR TO SIX

1 Put the garlic cloves in a mortar, add a pinch of salt and pound to a smooth paste with a pestle.

2 Transfer the garlic paste to a bowl. Add the egg yolks and whisk for about 30 seconds, until creamy. Whisk in the olive oil, drop by drop, until the mixture begins to thicken, then add the oil in a slow drizzle until the mixture is thick and creamy.

3 Beat in the lemon juice and seasoning to taste. Serve immediately or cover with clear film (plastic wrap) and chill in the refrigerator until ready to use. Allow the aioli to return to room temperature before serving.

4 large garlic cloves, peeled

2 egg yolks

250ml/8fl oz/1 cup extra virgin olive oil

15–30ml/1–2 tbsp lemon juice

Roasted Garlic Sauce

A roasted garlic sauce has plenty of robust flavour without the harshness of some uncooked garlic sauces and dressings. This one keeps well in the refrigerator for several days. Serve it as an accompaniment to barbecued burgers or sausages, grilled steaks, lamb chops or pork steaks – the possibilities are endless.

6 large heads of garlic

120ml/4fl oz/½ cup extra virgin olive oil

2 thick slices white bread, about 90g/3½oz

30–45ml/2–3 tbsp lemon juice

SERVES SIX TO EIGHT

1 Preheat the oven to 200°C/400°F/Gas 6. Slice the tops off the garlic and place the bulbs on a sheet of foil. Spoon over 30ml/2 tbsp of the oil and sprinkle with salt. Wrap the foil over the garlic and bake for 1 hour, until soft. Open out the foil and leave the garlic to cool.

2 Discard the crusts from the bread. Soak the bread in water for 1 minute, then squeeze dry and place in a food processor. Squeeze the garlic flesh into the processor. Process to a smooth paste.

3 Add 30ml/2 tbsp lemon juice with a little salt and pepper. With the machine running, gradually add the remaining oil in a thin stream to make a smooth paste. Check the seasoning, adding more lemon juice if needed. Turn into a bowl, cover and chill until required.

Watercress Sauce

This pretty green sauce is refreshingly tart and peppery. It is delicious served as an accompaniment to poached fish, or as a dip for simply grilled prawns (shrimp). Do not prepare the sauce more than a few hours ahead of serving, as the watercress will discolour the sauce. This peppery green sauce can also be made with rocket (arugula) leaves instead of the watercress.

SERVES SIX TO EIGHT

200g/7oz watercress leaves

300g/11oz/1¼ cups mayonnaise

15–30ml/1–2 tbsp freshly squeezed lemon juice

200g/7oz/scant 1 cup unsalted (sweet) butter

1 Remove the tough stems from the watercress leaves and finely chop the leaves by hand or in a food processor. Add the mayonnaise and the freshly squeezed lemon juice and process to mix.

2 Melt the unsalted butter, then add to the watercress mixture, a little at a time, processing or whisking in a bowl until the butter has been fully incorporated and the sauce is thick and smooth. Season to taste with salt and pepper, then cover and chill in the refrigerator for at least an hour before serving.

EXTRAS

Garlic makes a delicious addition to this sauce. Peel and finely chop 1–2 garlic cloves and combine with the chopped watercress leaves, mayonnaise and lemon juice, before adding the melted butter in step 2.

Shallots in Balsamic Vinegar

These whole shallots cooked in balsamic vinegar and herbs are a modern variation on pickled onions, but they have a much more gentle, smooth flavour. They are delicious served with cold pies, meats and cheese. A combination of bay leaves and thyme are used here but rosemary, oregano or marjoram sprigs would work just as well.

SERVES SIX

1 Put the unpeeled shallots in a bowl, cover with boiling water and leave for 2 minutes for the skins to loosen. Drain and peel the shallots, leaving them whole.

2 Put the sugar, bay leaves or thyme and vinegar in a heavy pan and bring to the boil. Add the shallots, cover and simmer gently for about 40 minutes, until the shallots are just tender.

3 Transfer the mixture to a sterilized jar, seal and label, then store in a cool, dark place. Alternatively, drain and transfer to a serving dish. Leave to cool, then chill until ready to serve.

500g/1¼lb shallots

30ml/2 tbsp muscovado (molasses) sugar

several bay leaves or fresh thyme sprigs

300ml/½ pint/ 1¼ cups balsamic vinegar

Barbecue Sauce

A wide selection of ready-made barbecue sauces are available in the supermarkets, but they really don't compare with the home-made variety. This 10-minute version can be used to transform baked or grilled chicken, sausages or fish into an interesting meal that needs no more than a mixed salad and baked potatoes as accompaniments.

SERVES FOUR TO SIX

1 Tip the cans of chopped tomatoes with herbs or garlic into a medium, heavy pan and add the finely chopped onion, black treacle and Worcestershire sauce.

2 Bring to the boil and cook, uncovered, until the mixture is thickened and pulpy, stirring frequently with a wooden spoon to stop the sauce catching on the base of the pan. Season lightly with salt and plenty of freshly ground black pepper and transfer to a serving dish or jug (pitcher). Serve the sauce warm or cold.

2 x 400g/14 oz cans chopped tomatoes with herbs or garlic

1 onion, finely chopped

15ml/1 tbsp black treacle (molasses)

45ml/3 tbsp Worcestershire sauce

Mixed Herb and Peppercorn Sauce

This lovely, refreshing sauce relies on absolutely fresh herbs (any combination will do) and good-quality olive oil for its fabulous flavour. Make it a day in advance, to allow the flavours to mingle. Serve the sauce with simply cooked fish such as salmon or with grilled beef or lamb steaks.

SERVES FOUR TO SIX

1 Crush the cumin seeds using a mortar and pestle. Alternatively, put the seeds in a small bowl and pound them with the end of a rolling pin. Add the pink or green peppercorns and pound a little to break them up slightly.

2 Remove any tough stalks from the herbs. Put the herbs in a food processor with the cumin seeds, peppercorns, oil and salt and process until the herbs are finely chopped, scraping the sauce down from the sides of the bowl if necessary.

3 Turn the sauce into a small serving dish, cover with clear film (plastic wrap) and chill until ready to serve.

10ml/2 tsp cumin seeds

15ml/1 tbsp pink or green peppercorns in brine, drained and rinsed

25g/1oz/1 cup fresh mixed herbs, such as parsley, mint, chives and coriander (cilantro)

45ml/3 tbsp lemon-infused olive oil

Index

A

aioli, 246

almonds

almond cookies, 213

almond cigars, 211

blueberry and almond tart, 200

anchovy and roasted pepper salad, 153

apples

apple shiner, 22

hot blackberry and apple soufflé, 193

leafy apple lift-off, 18

apricot and ginger gratin, 191

artichokes

deep-fried artichokes, 133

globe artichokes with green beans
and garlic dressing, 142

arugula *see* rocket

asparagus

asparagus, bacon and leaf salad, 152

asparagus with lemon sauce, 126

atole, 30

aubergines

aubergines with cheese sauce, 94

baba ghanoush, 37

tomato and aubergine gratin, 132

avgolemono, 54

avocados

avocado soup, 52

pink grapefruit and avocado
salad, 147

B

baba ghanoush, 37

bacon

asparagus, bacon and leaf salad, 152

bacon-rolled enokitake
mushrooms, 44

scallops with fennel and bacon, 74

baguette, French, 226

baked custard with burnt sugar, 176

bananas

baked bananas with ice cream and
toffee sauce, 201

banana and maple flip, 29

strawberry and banana smoothie, 26

barbecue sauce, 250

basil

basil oil, 13

tomato, bean and fried basil
salad, 145

beans

butter bean, sun-dried tomato and
pesto soup, 60

globe artichokes with green beans
and garlic dressing, 142

mixed bean and tomato chilli, 104

rosemary risotto with borlotti
beans, 118

tomato, bean and fried basil
salad, 145

béchamel sauce, 12

C

cappelletti in broth, 56

caramel custard, baked, 178

caramel and pecan terrine, 167

carrots

carrot revitalizer, 21

Moroccan carrot salad, 149

Moroccan date, orange and carrot
salad, 146

purple pep, 21

tagliatelle with vegetable
ribbons, 113

cauliflower with garlic crumbs, 128

beef

beef patties with onions and
peppers, 78

steak with warm tomato salsa, 79

stock, 10

beet *see* beetroot

beetroot

beetroot with fresh mint, 141

horseradish and beetroot sauce, 242

purple pep, 21

Middle Eastern pickle, 241

bell peppers *see* peppers

biscuits, 207, 212–14

blackberries

blackberry ice cream, 161

bramble jelly, 236

hot blackberry and apple soufflé, 193

blackcurrant sorbet, 158

blueberry and almond tart, 200

borlotti beans, rosemary risotto
with, 118

bouquet garni, 11

bramble jelly, 236

breads, 220–33

broad beans

pancetta and broad bean risotto, 119

broiling see grilling

brownies, rich chocolate, 208

bubble and squeak, 135

butter bean, sun-dried tomato and
pesto soup, 60